For commercial use permissions, reproduction or other inquiries, please contact:
Alex.Kristian.h@gmail.com.
ISBN: 9798863745817
Published by Amazon Kindle.

THIS BOOK BELONGS TO

Color Testing Page

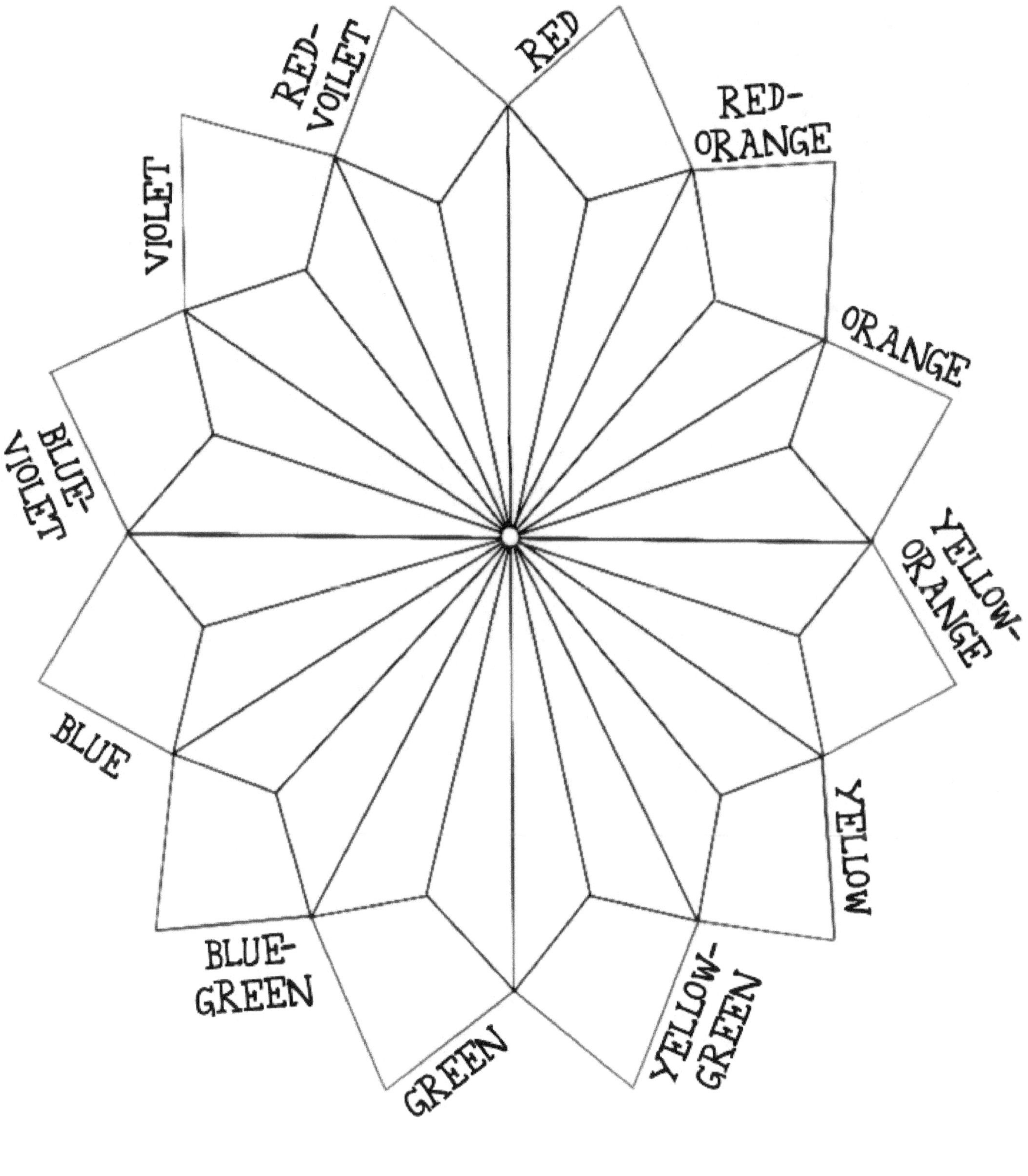

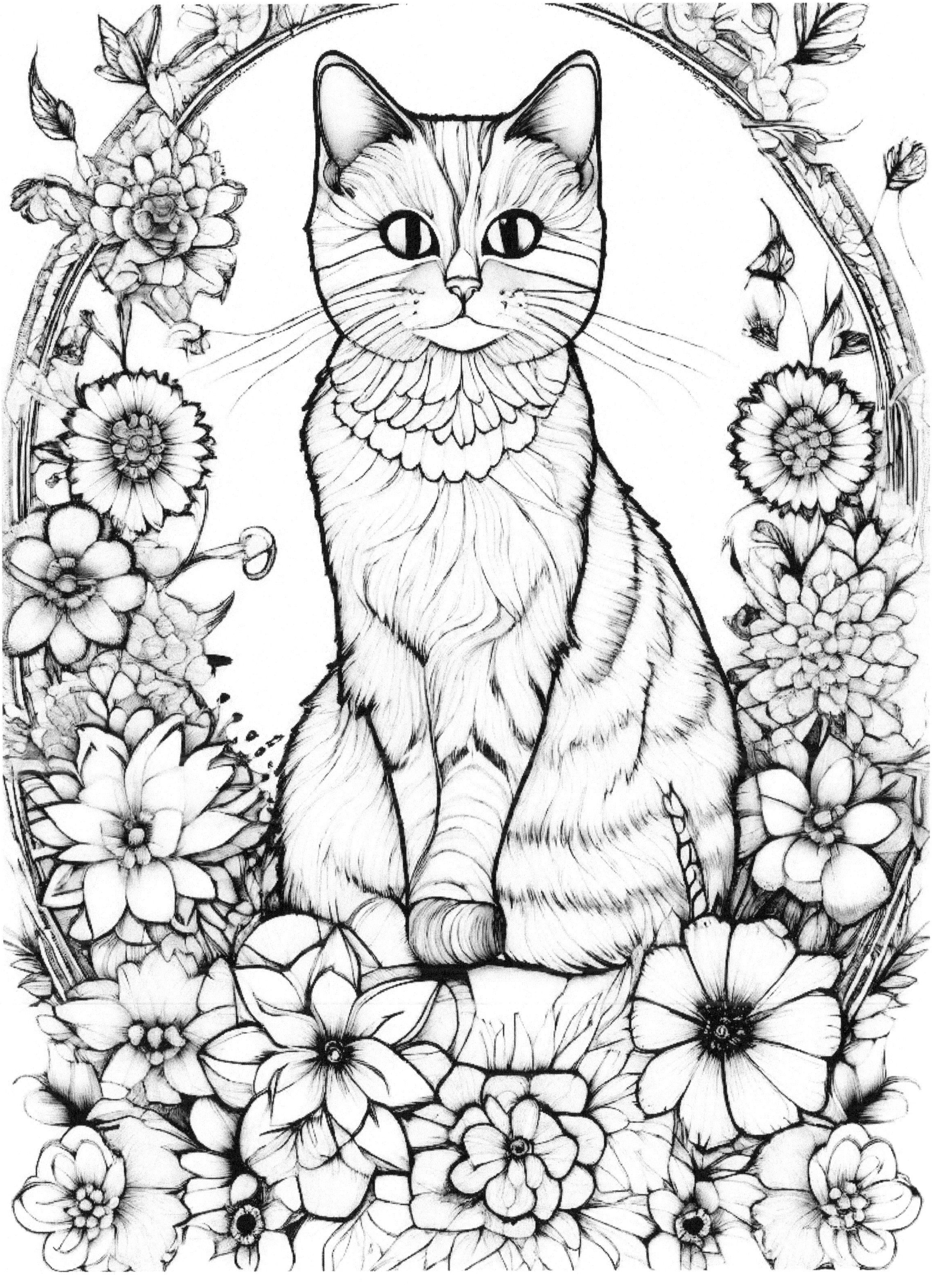

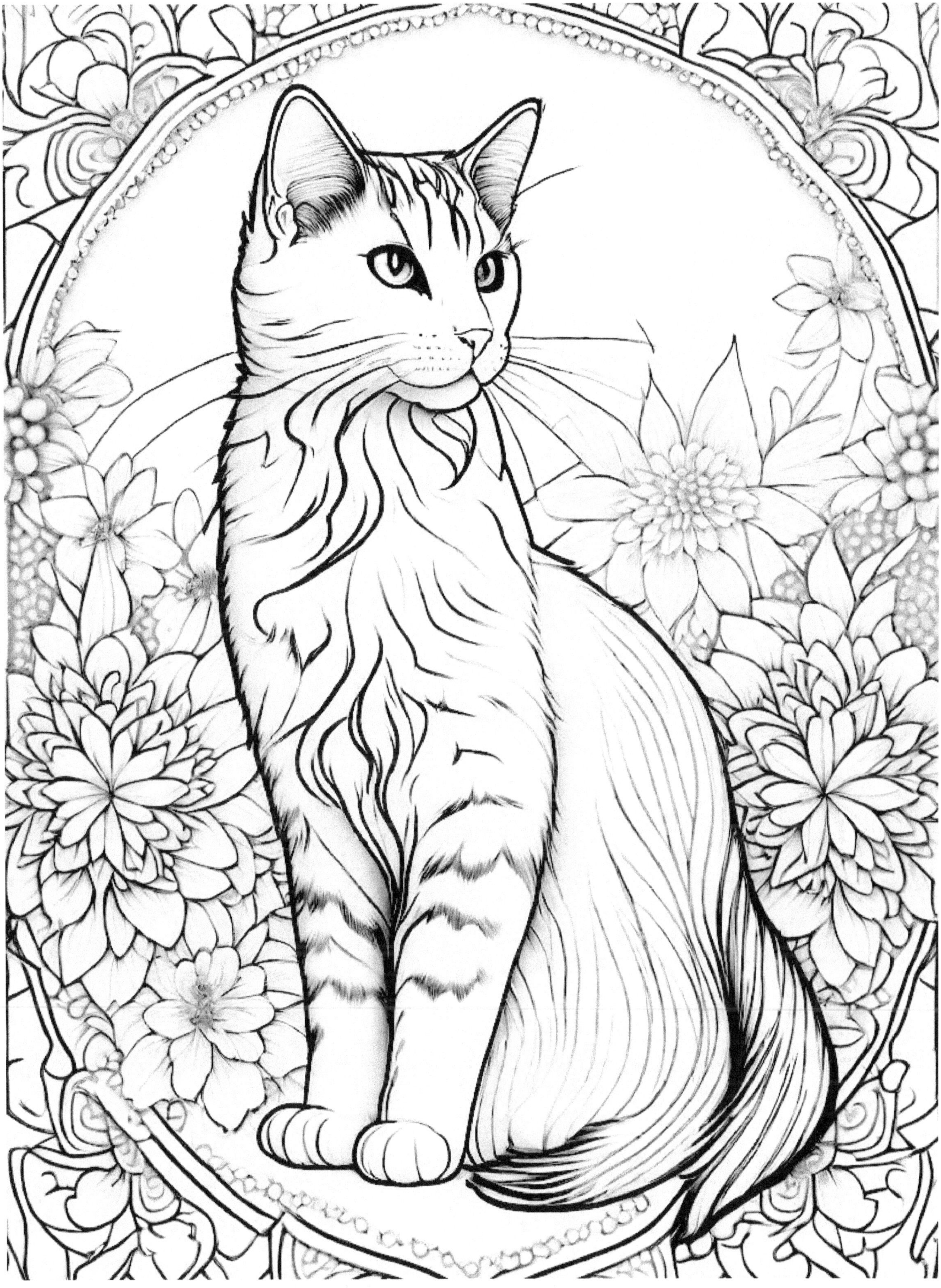

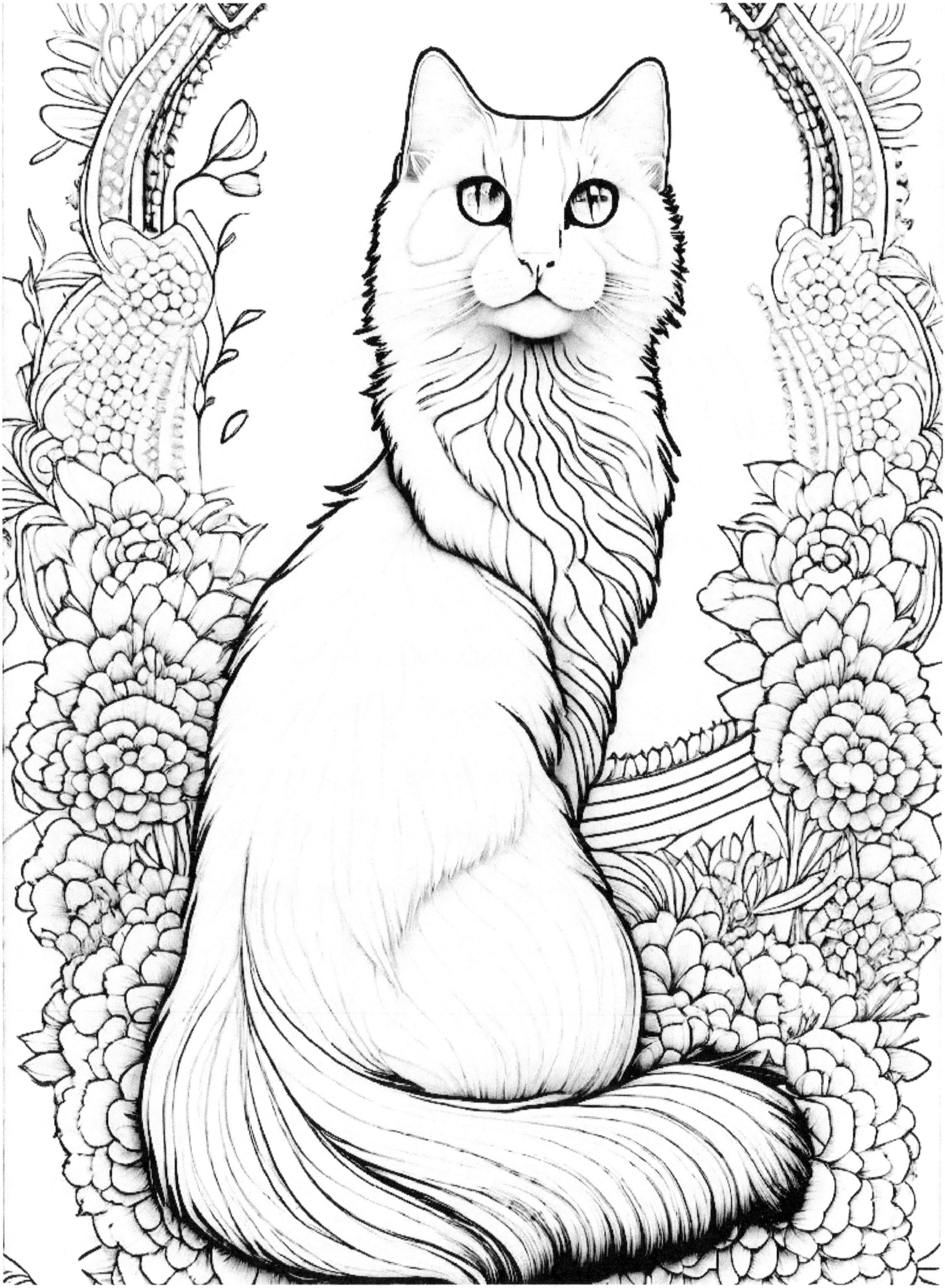

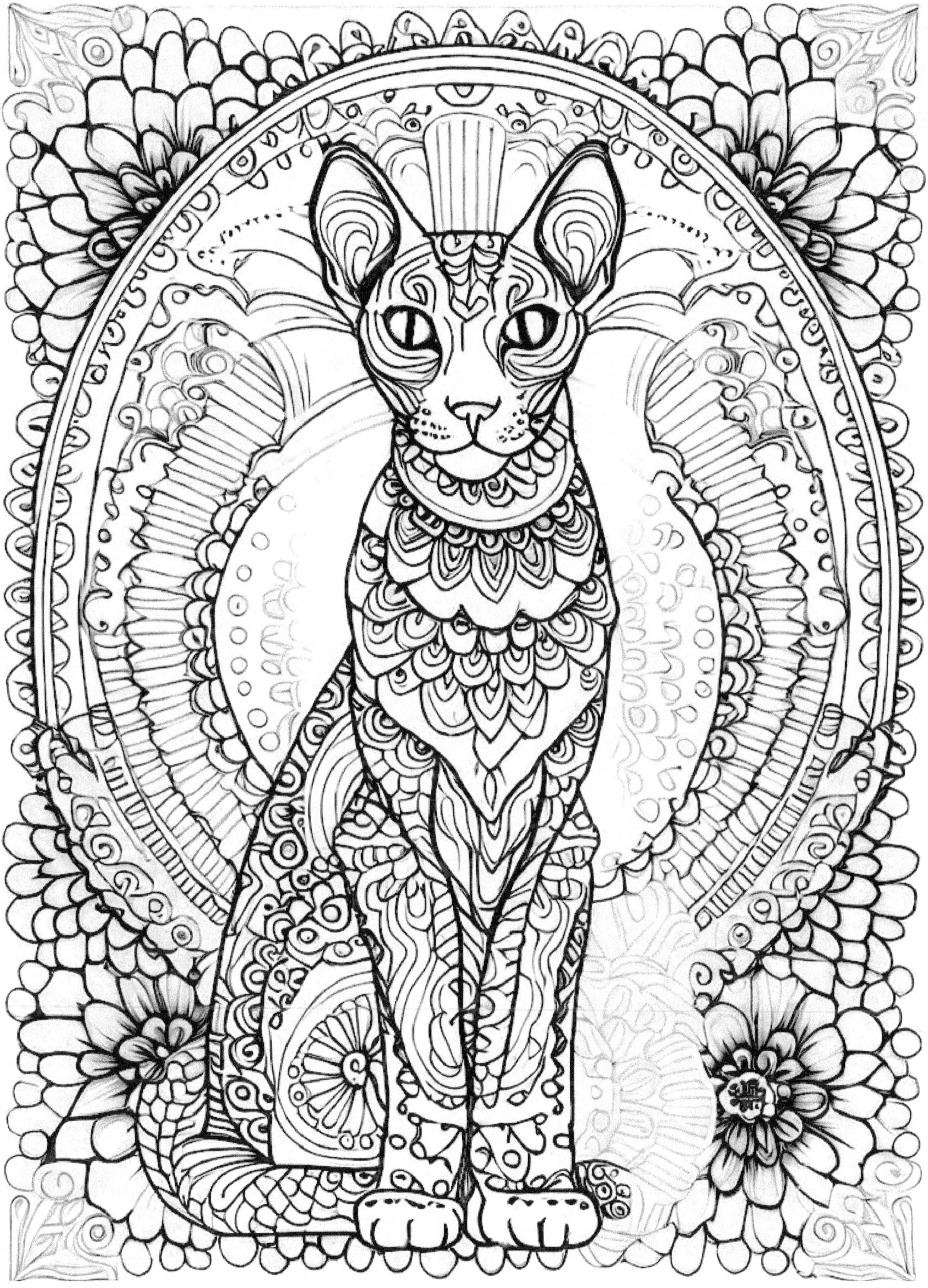

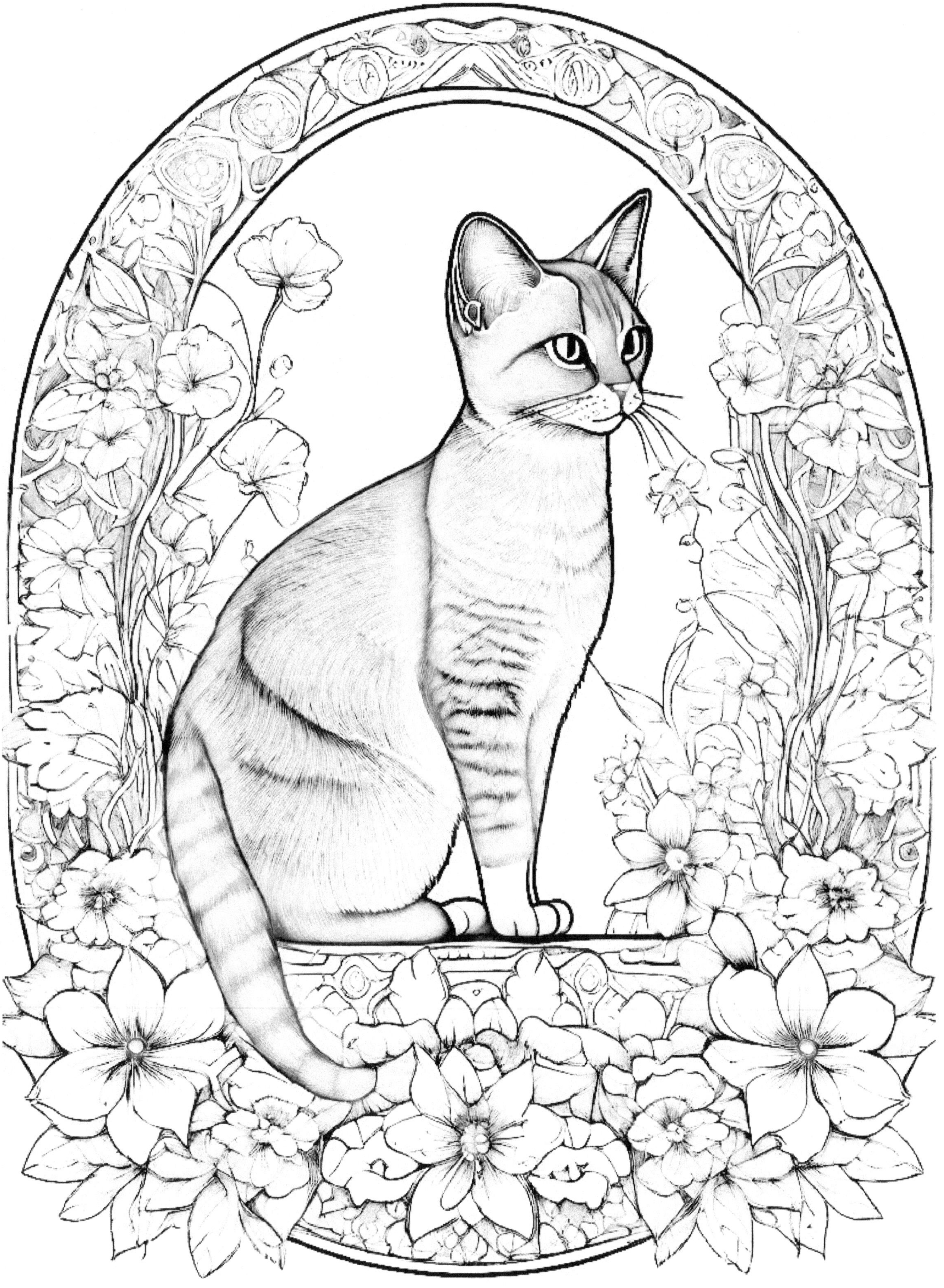

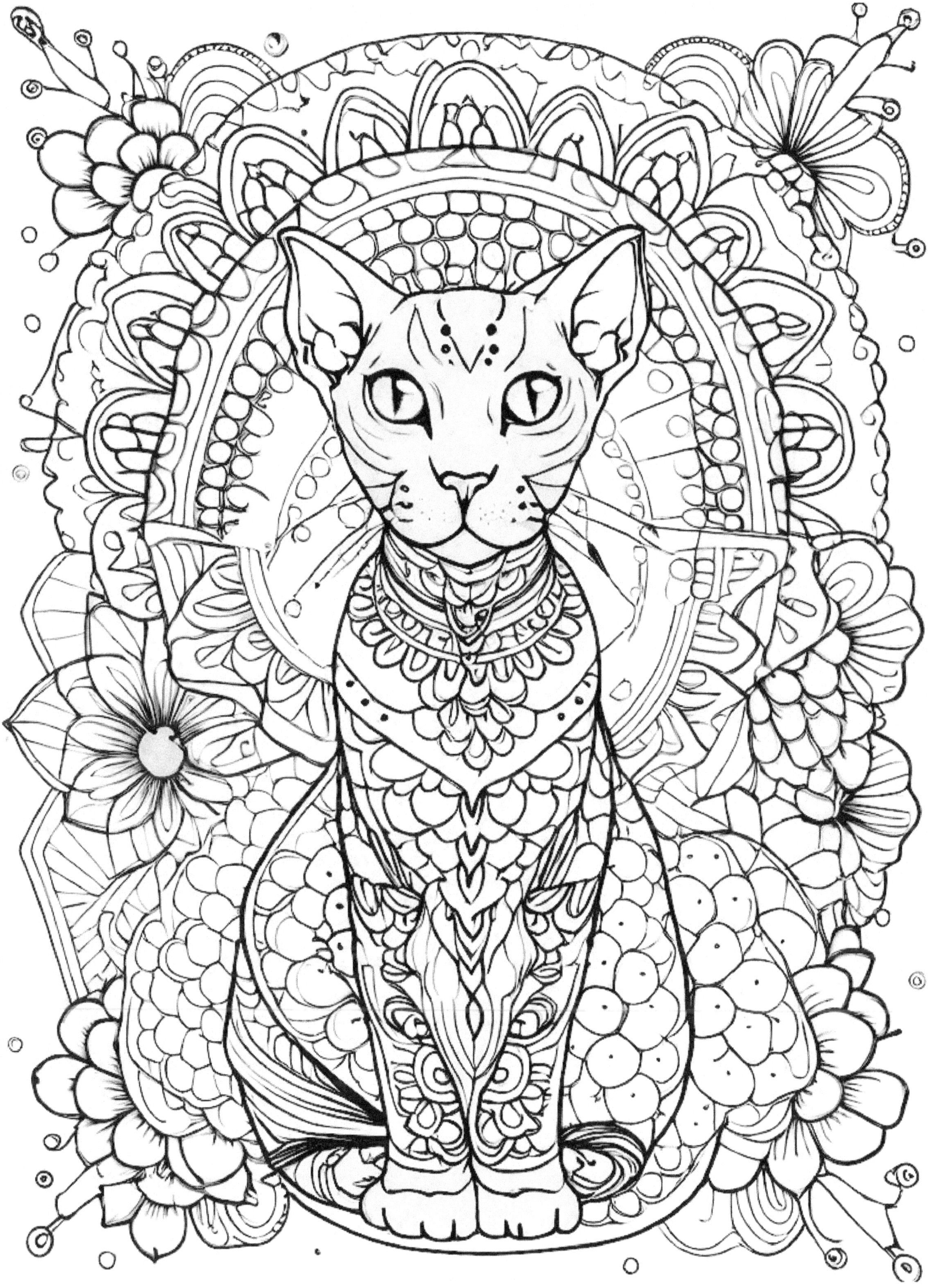

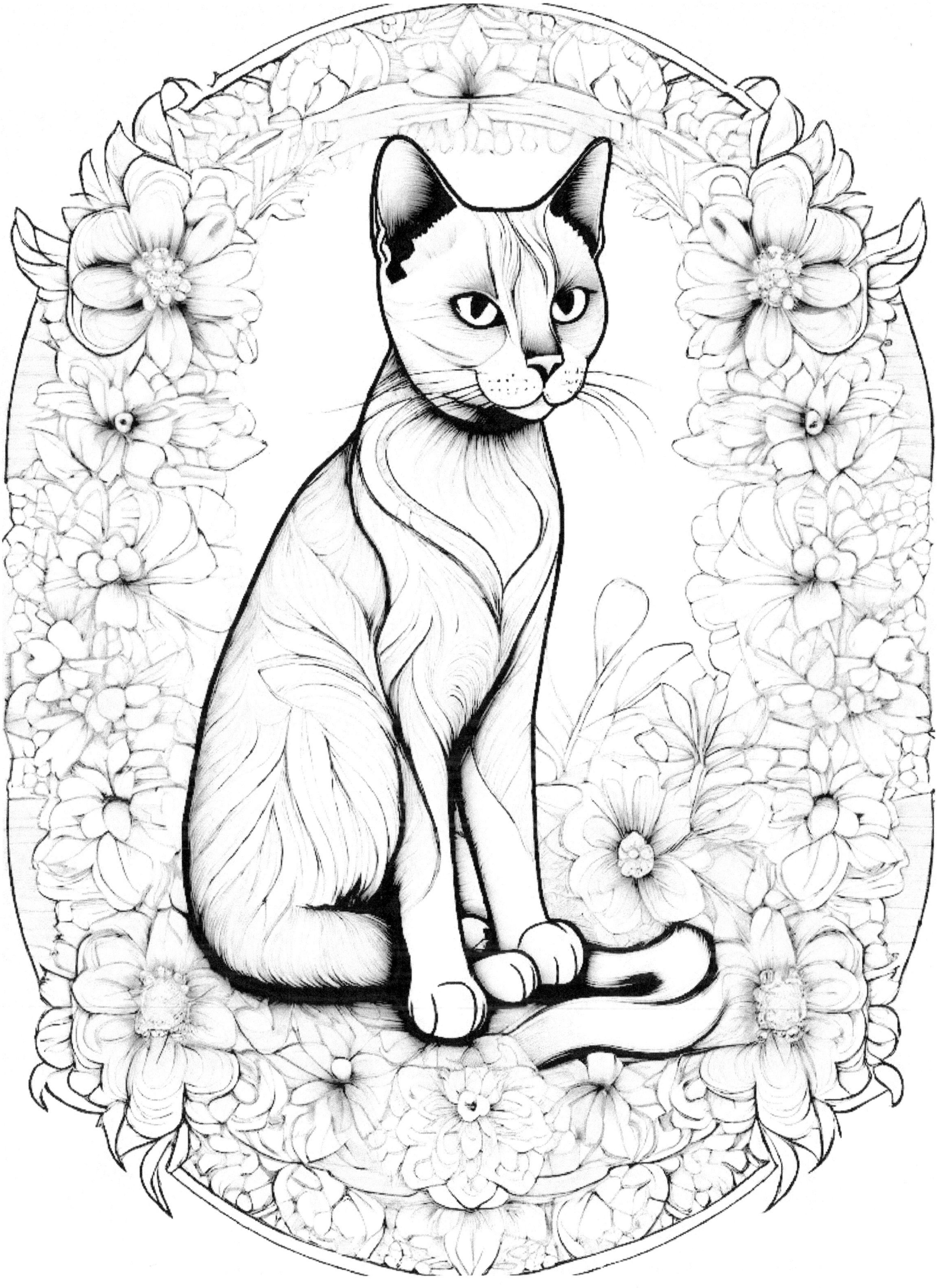

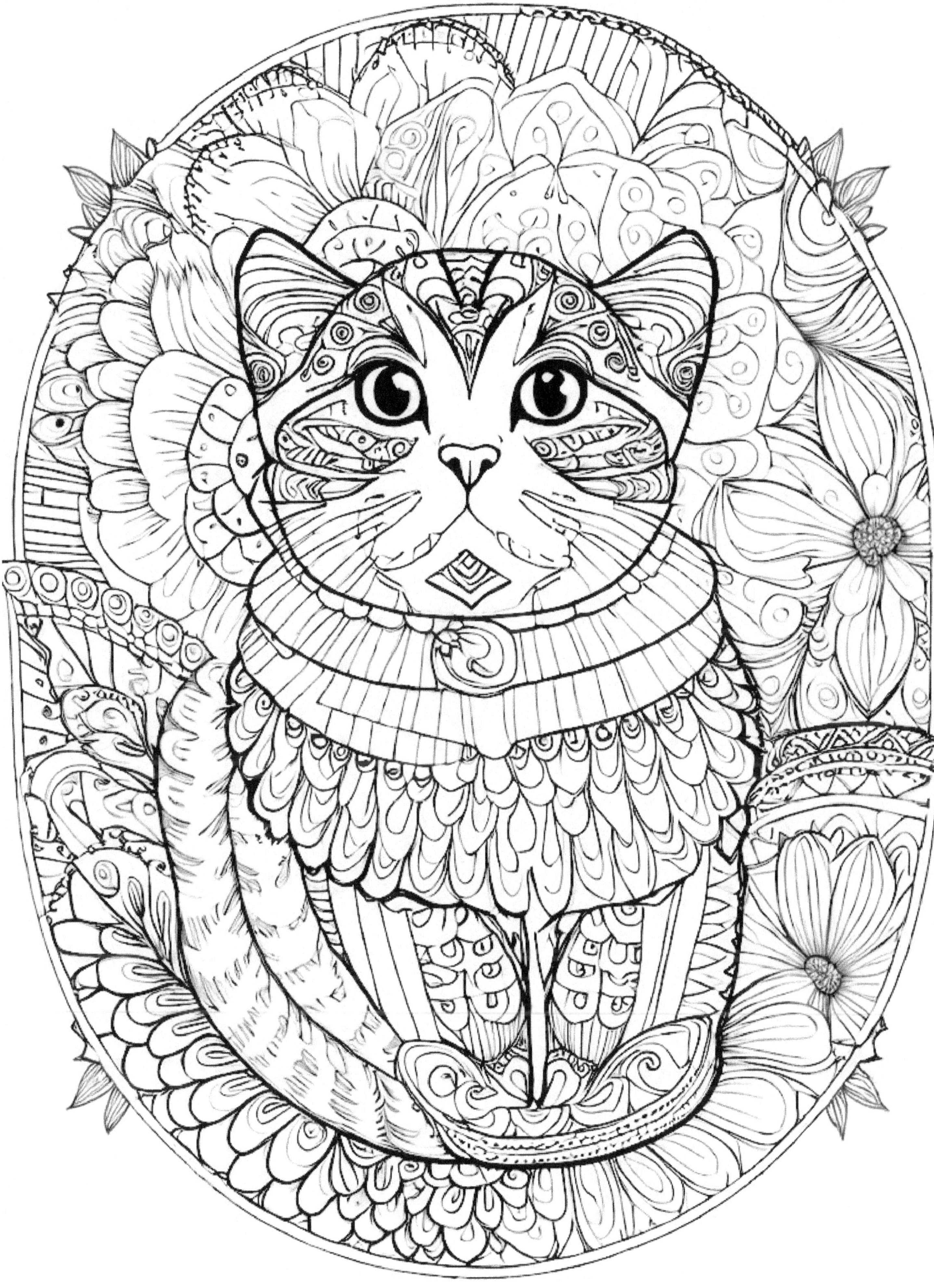

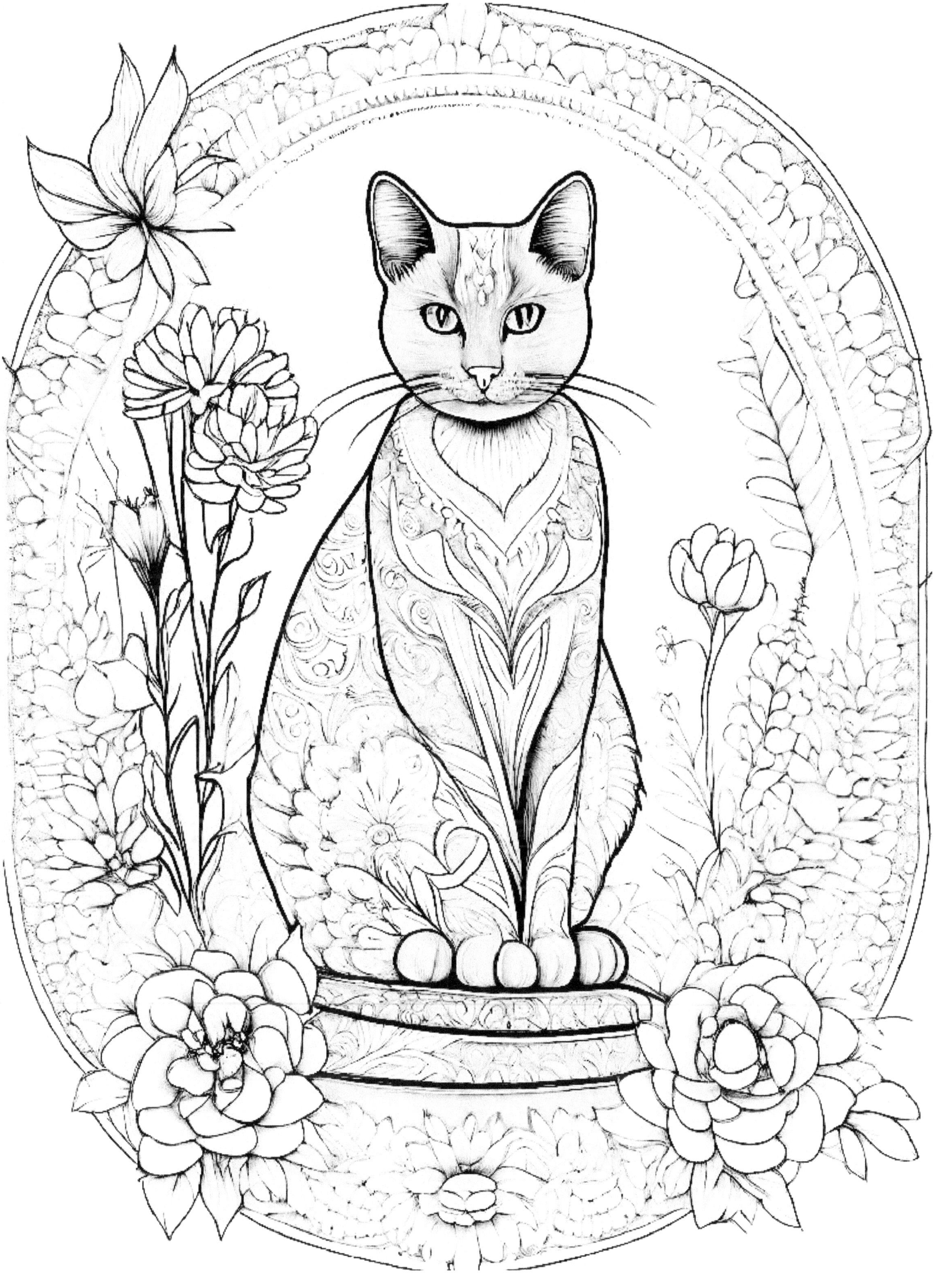

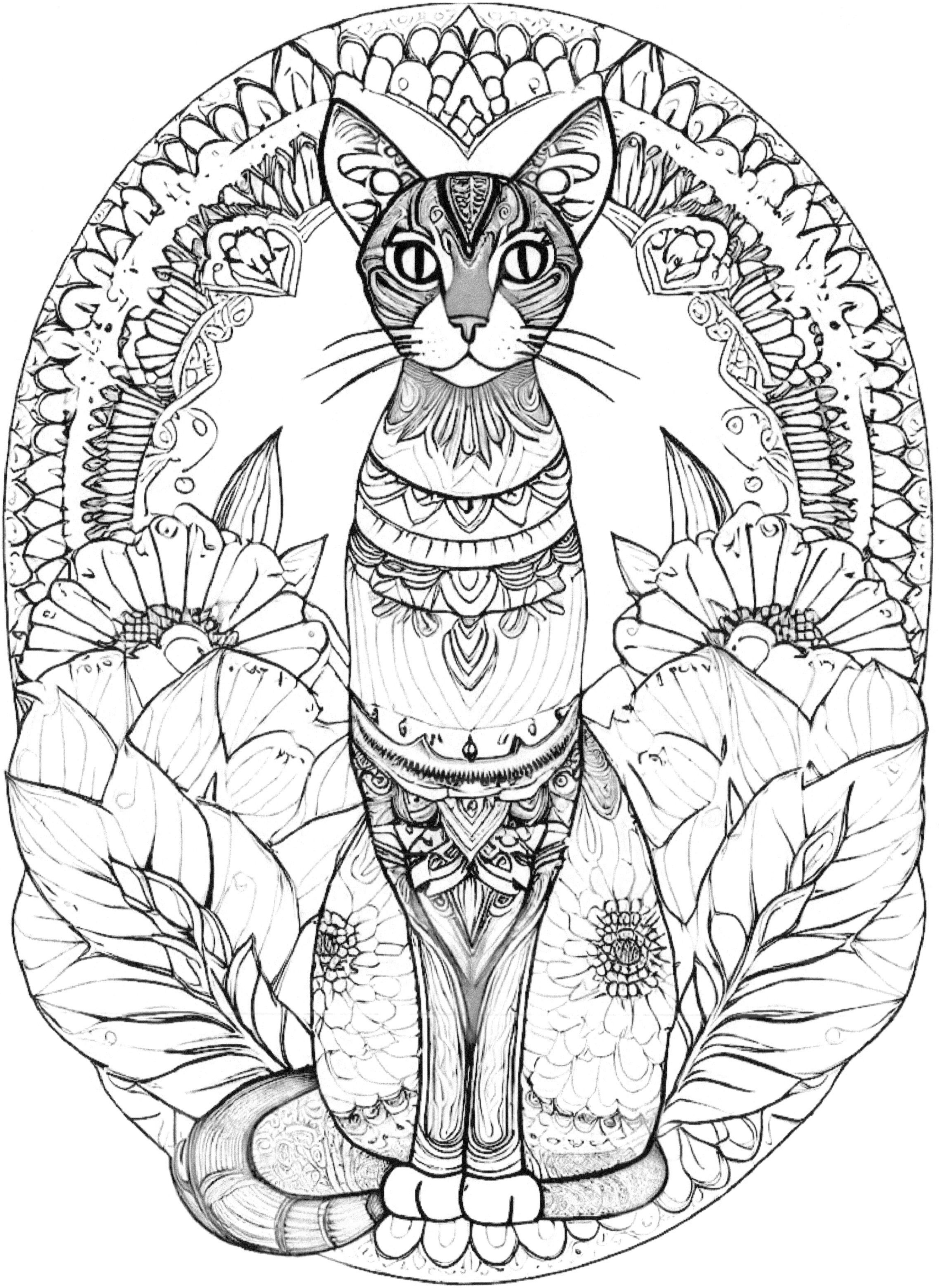

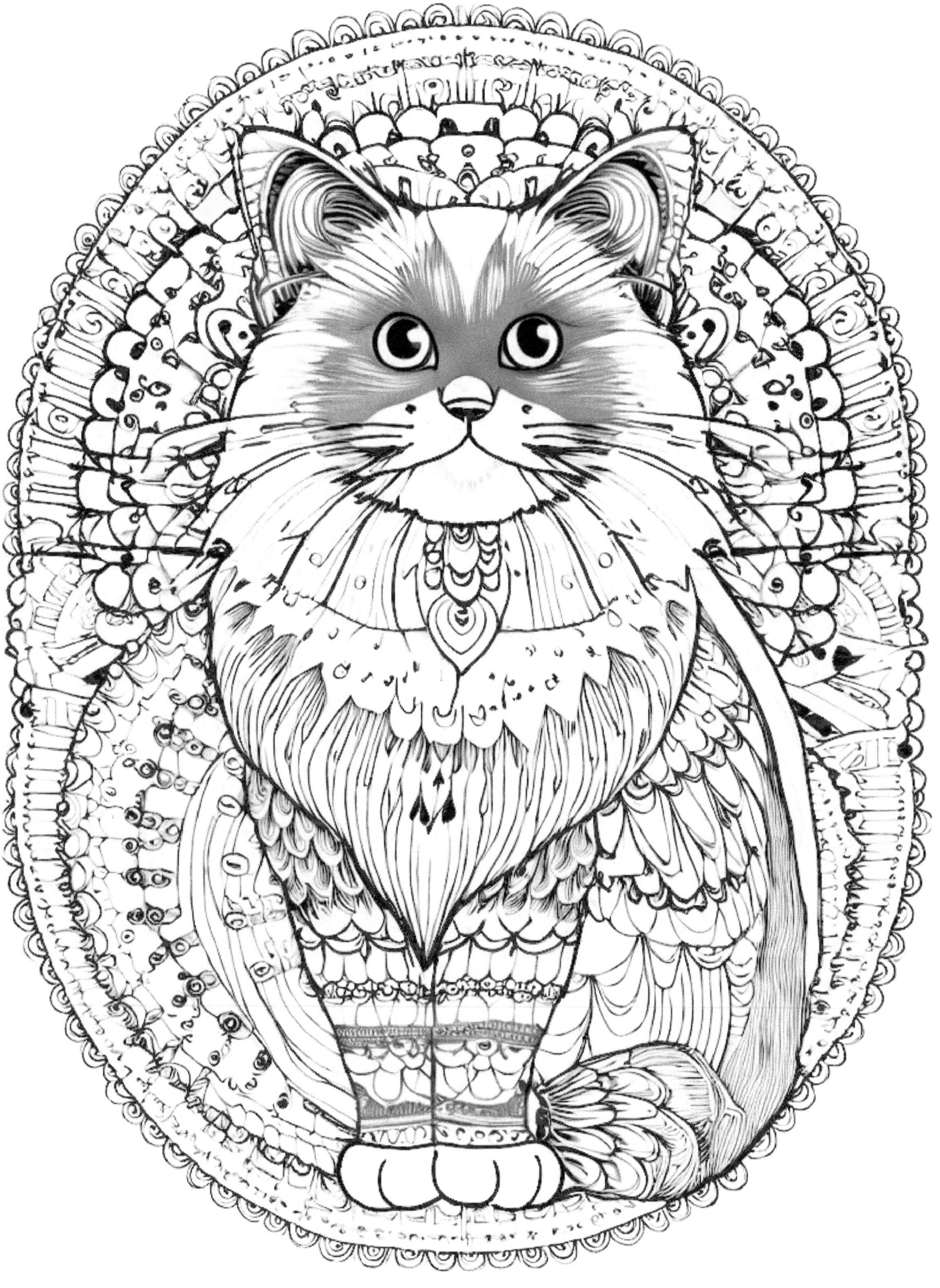

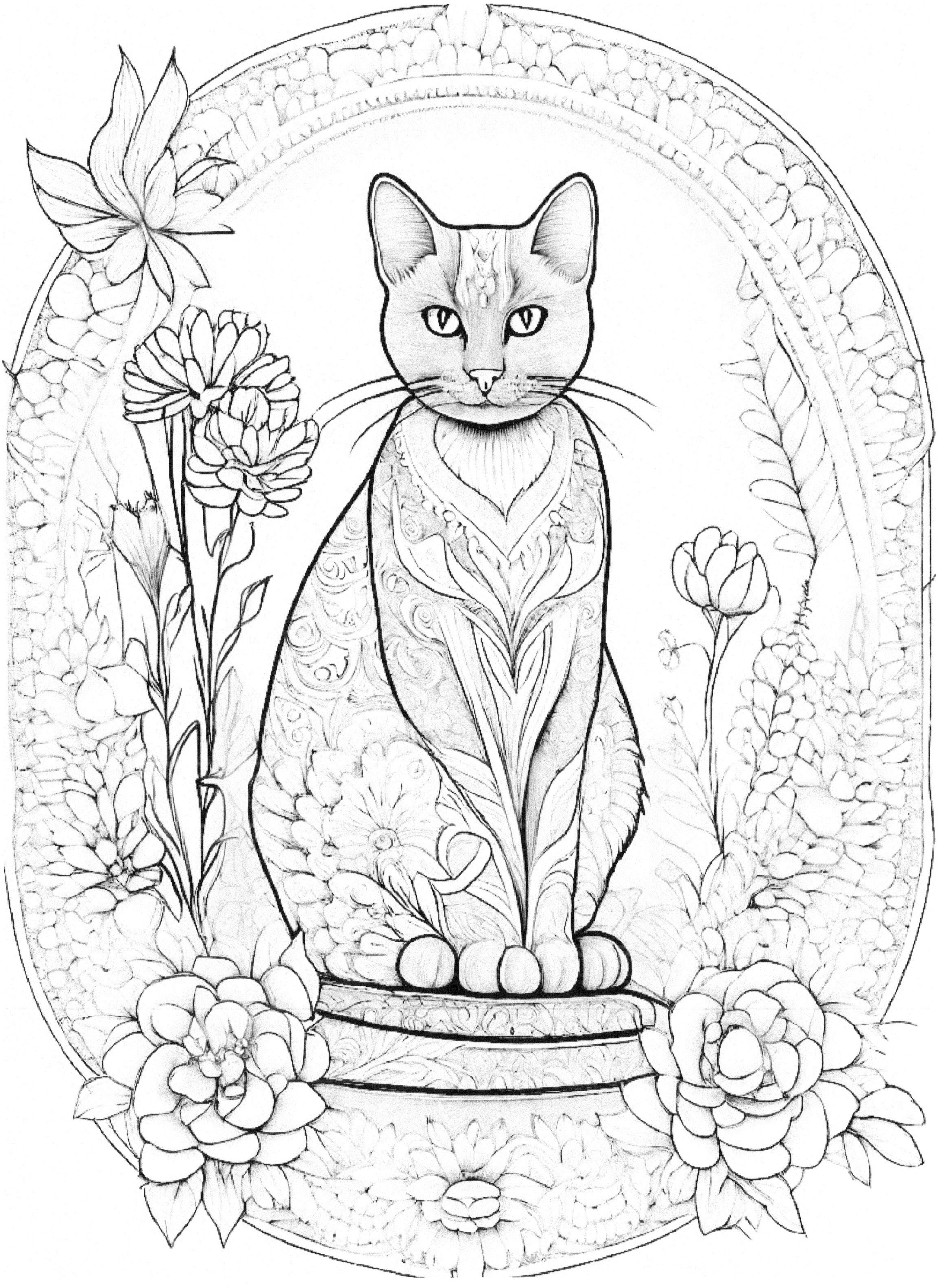

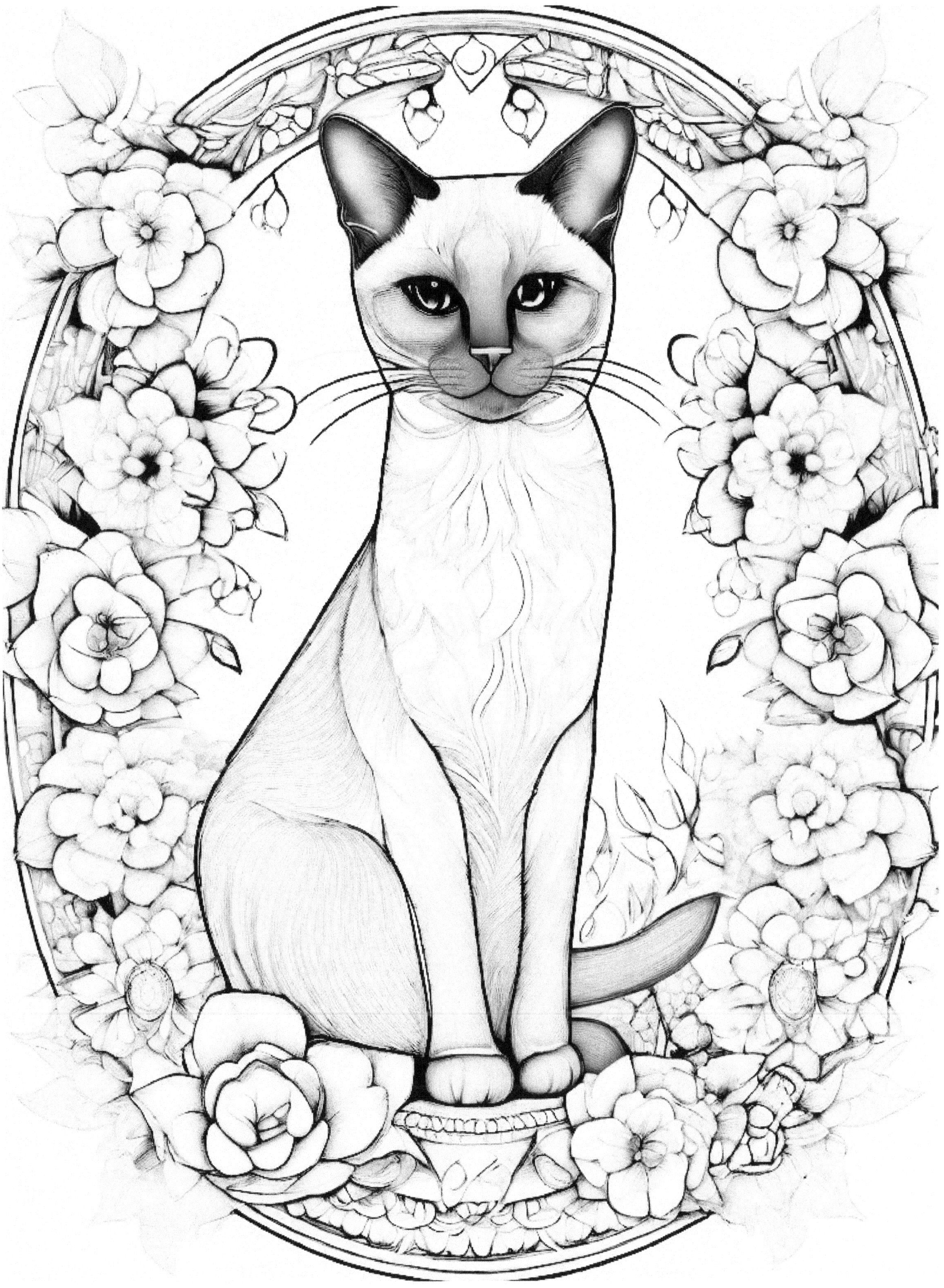

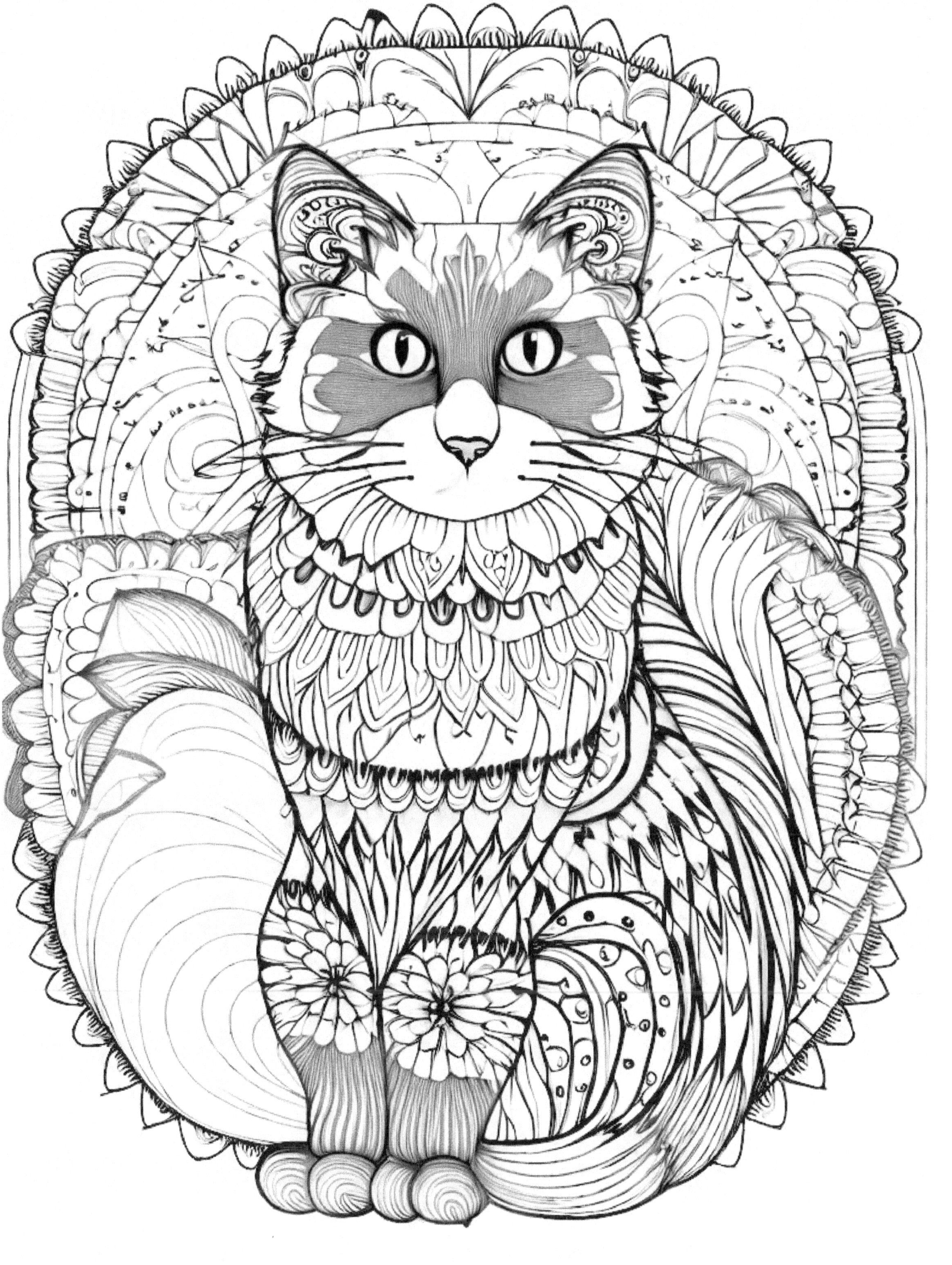

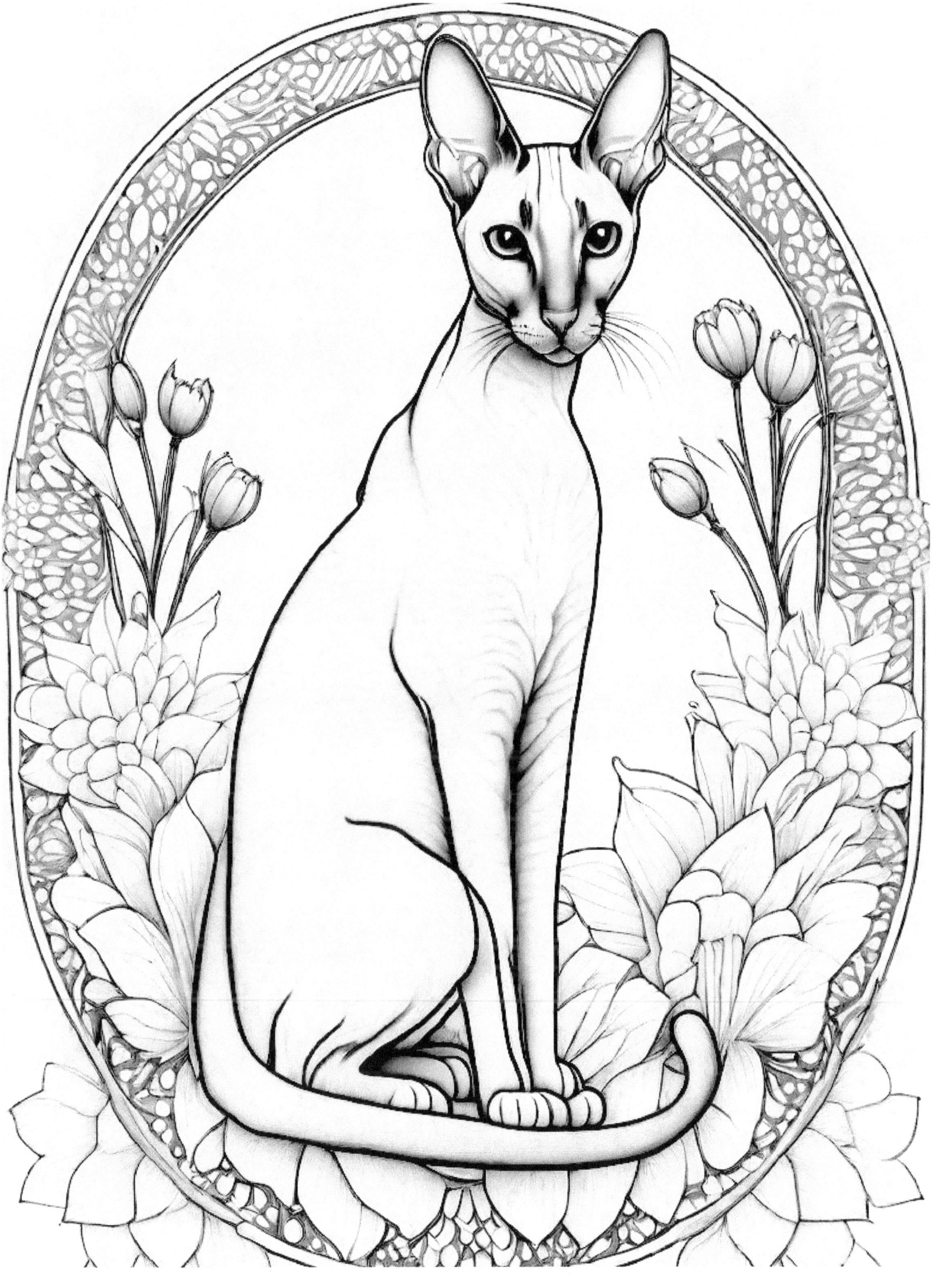

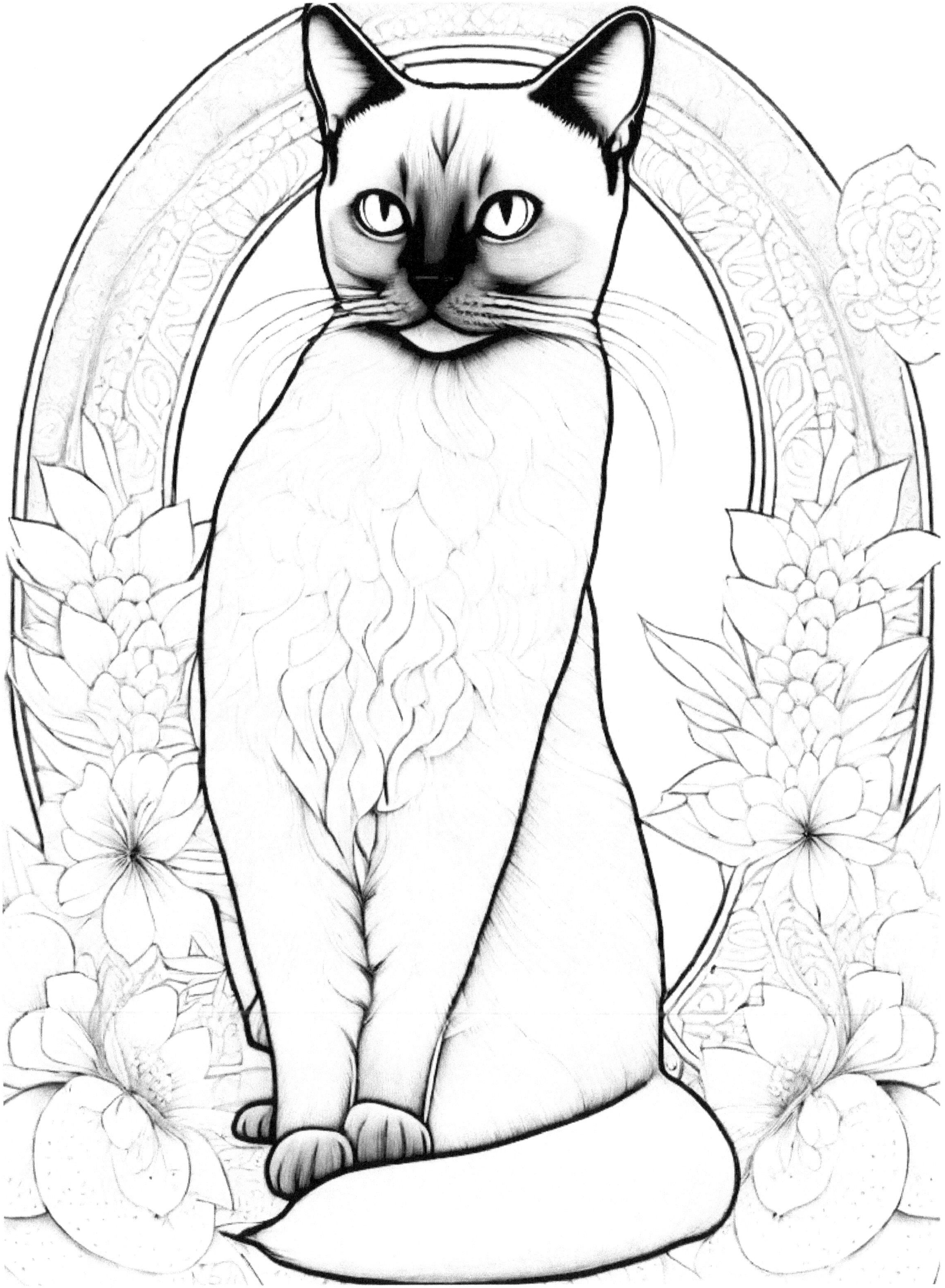

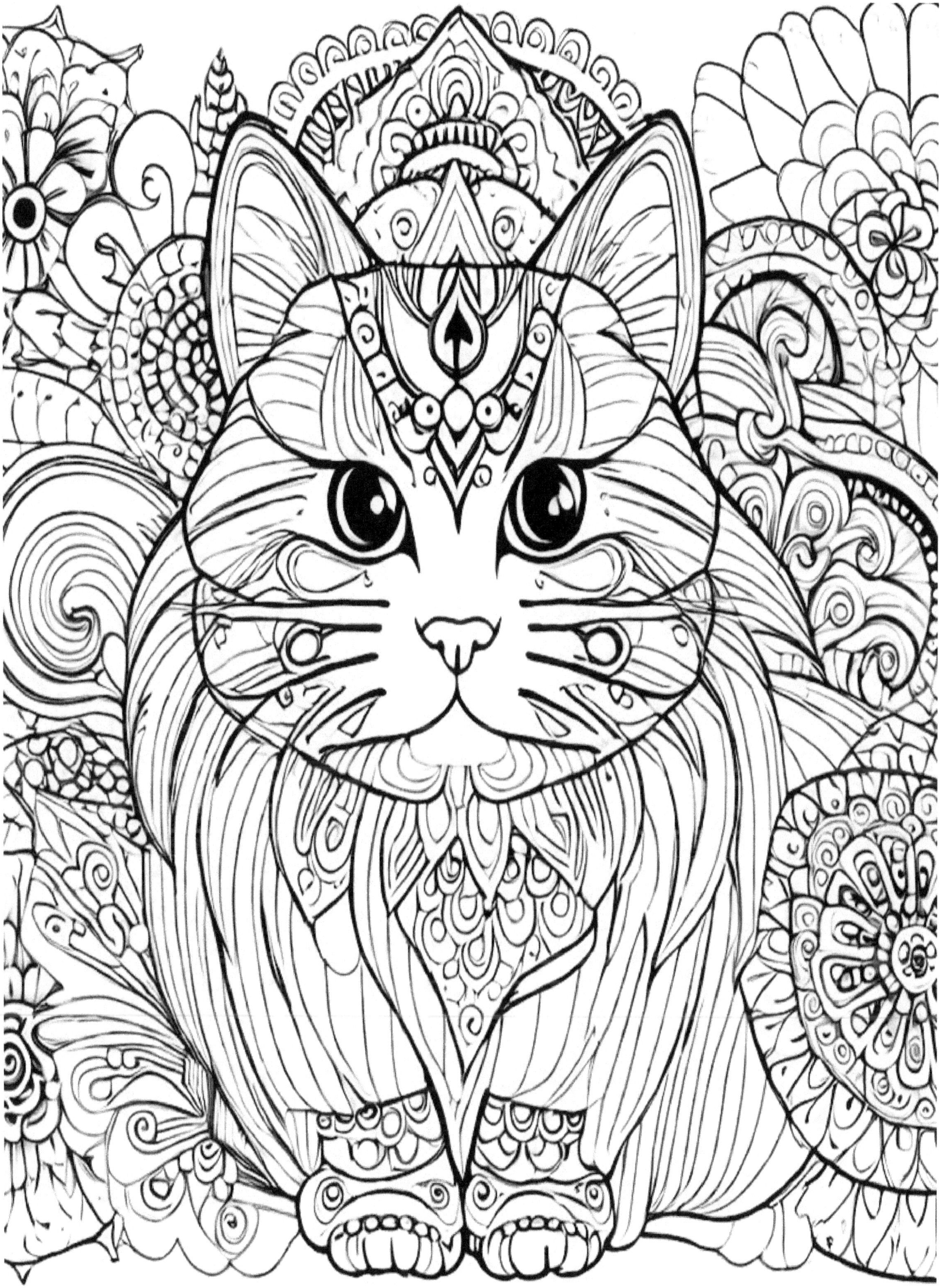

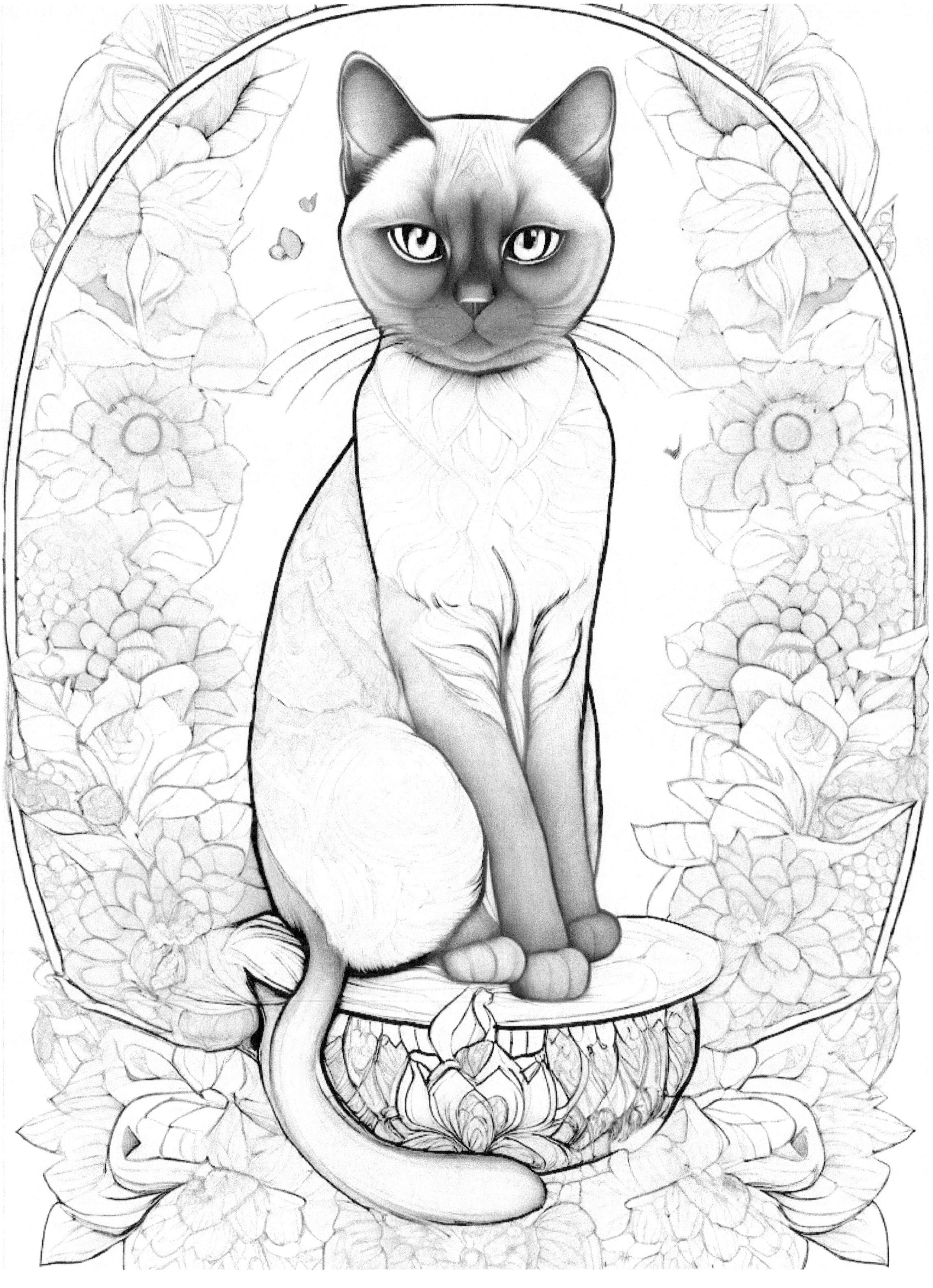

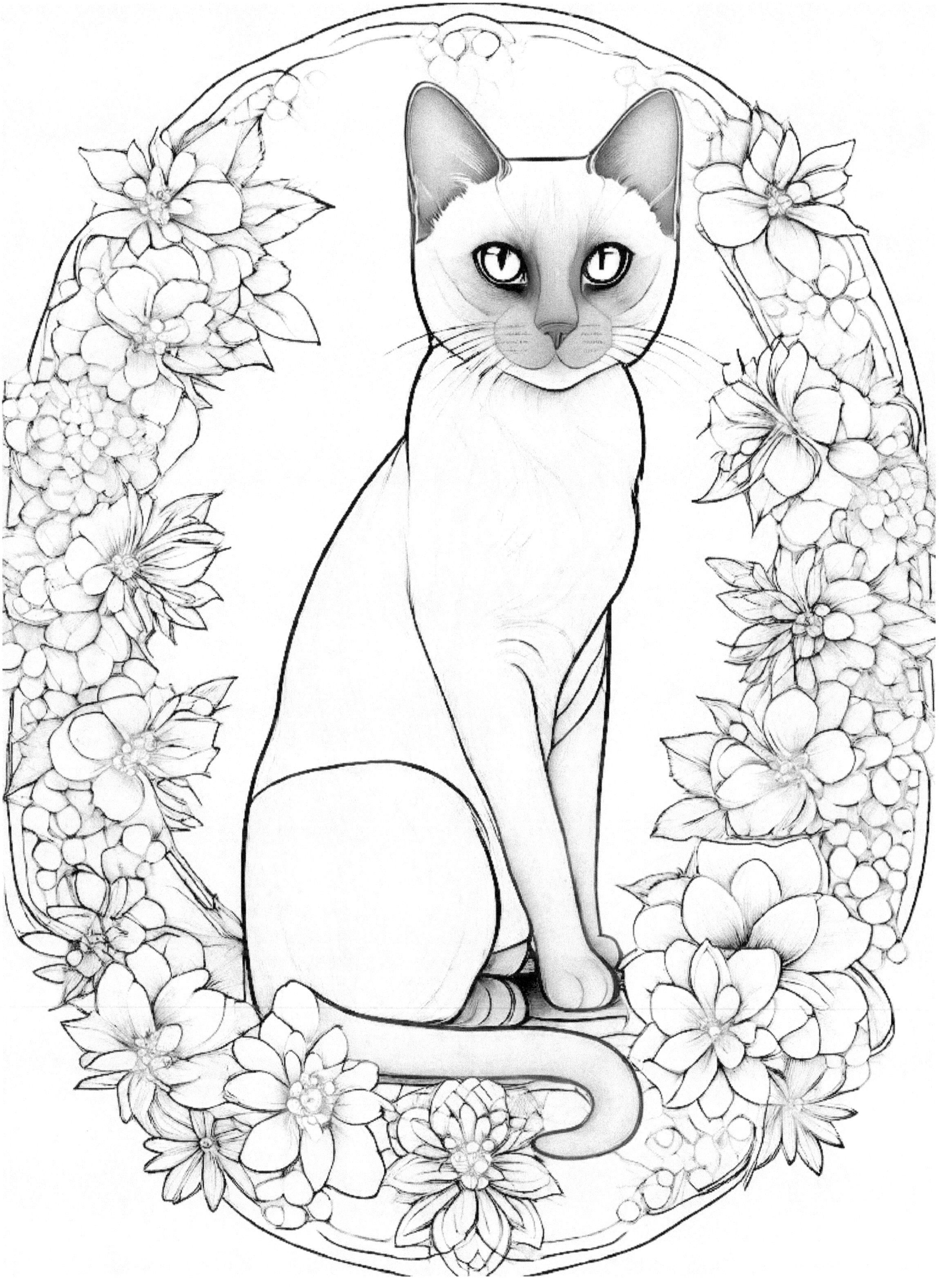

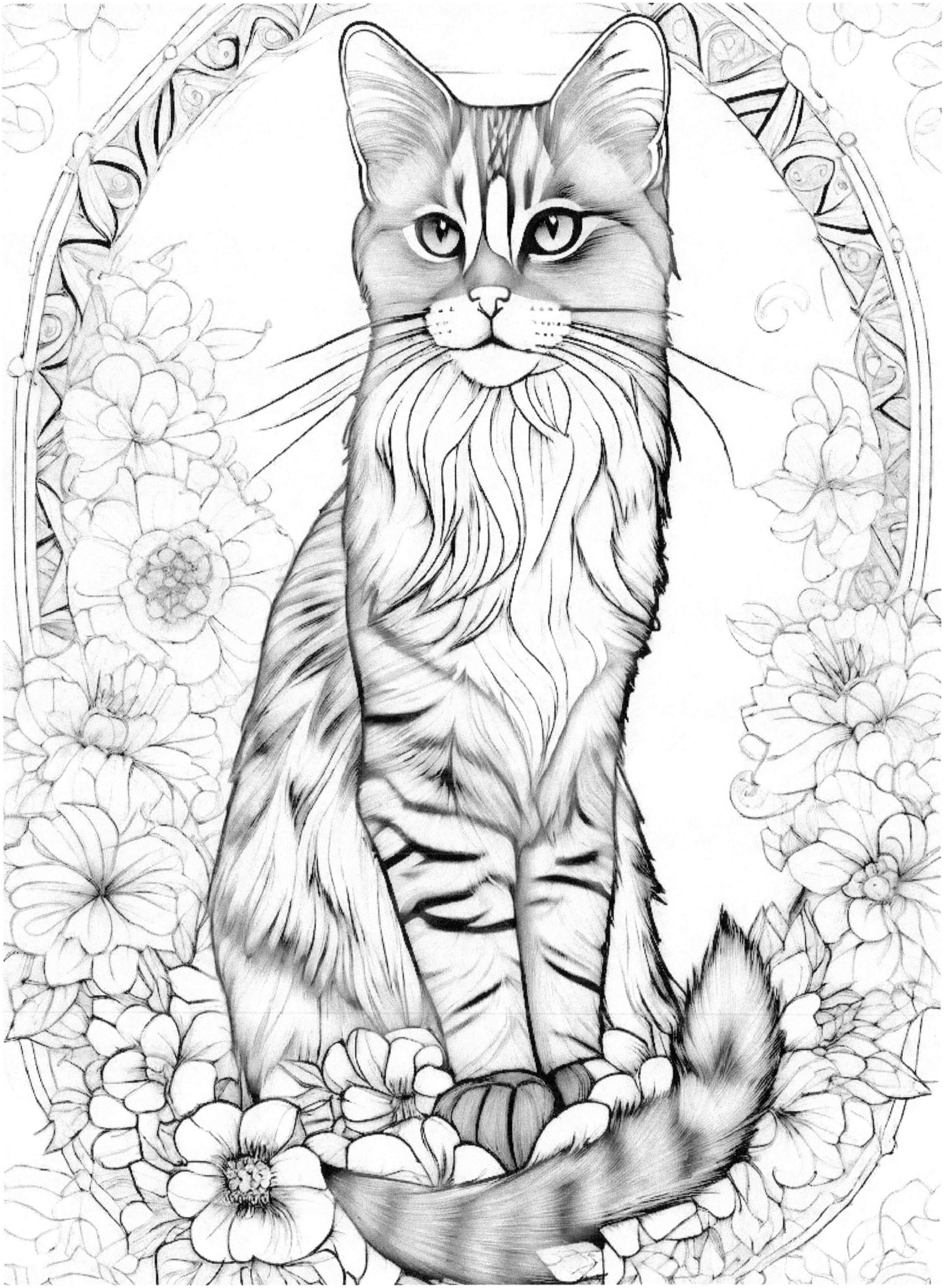

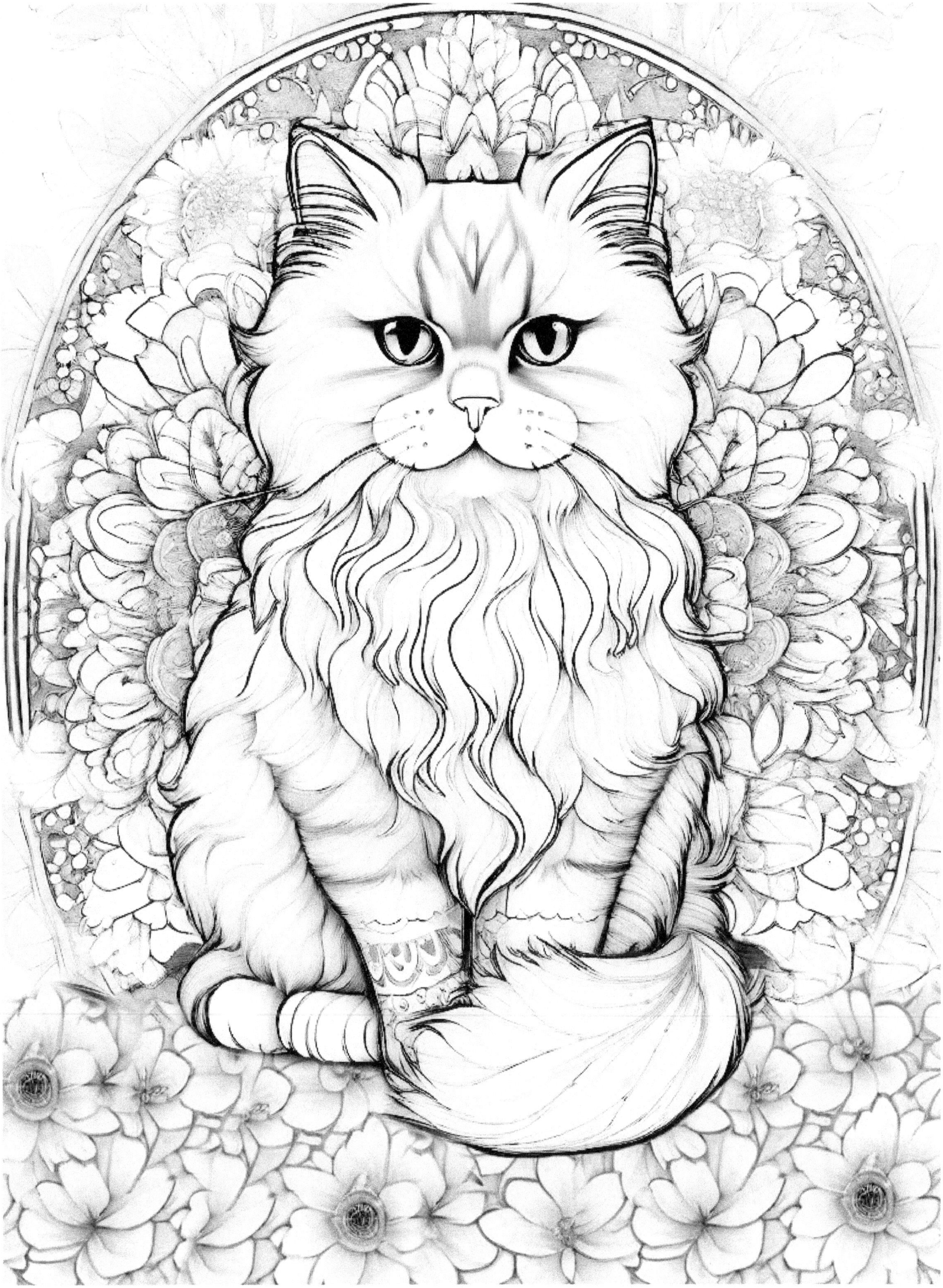

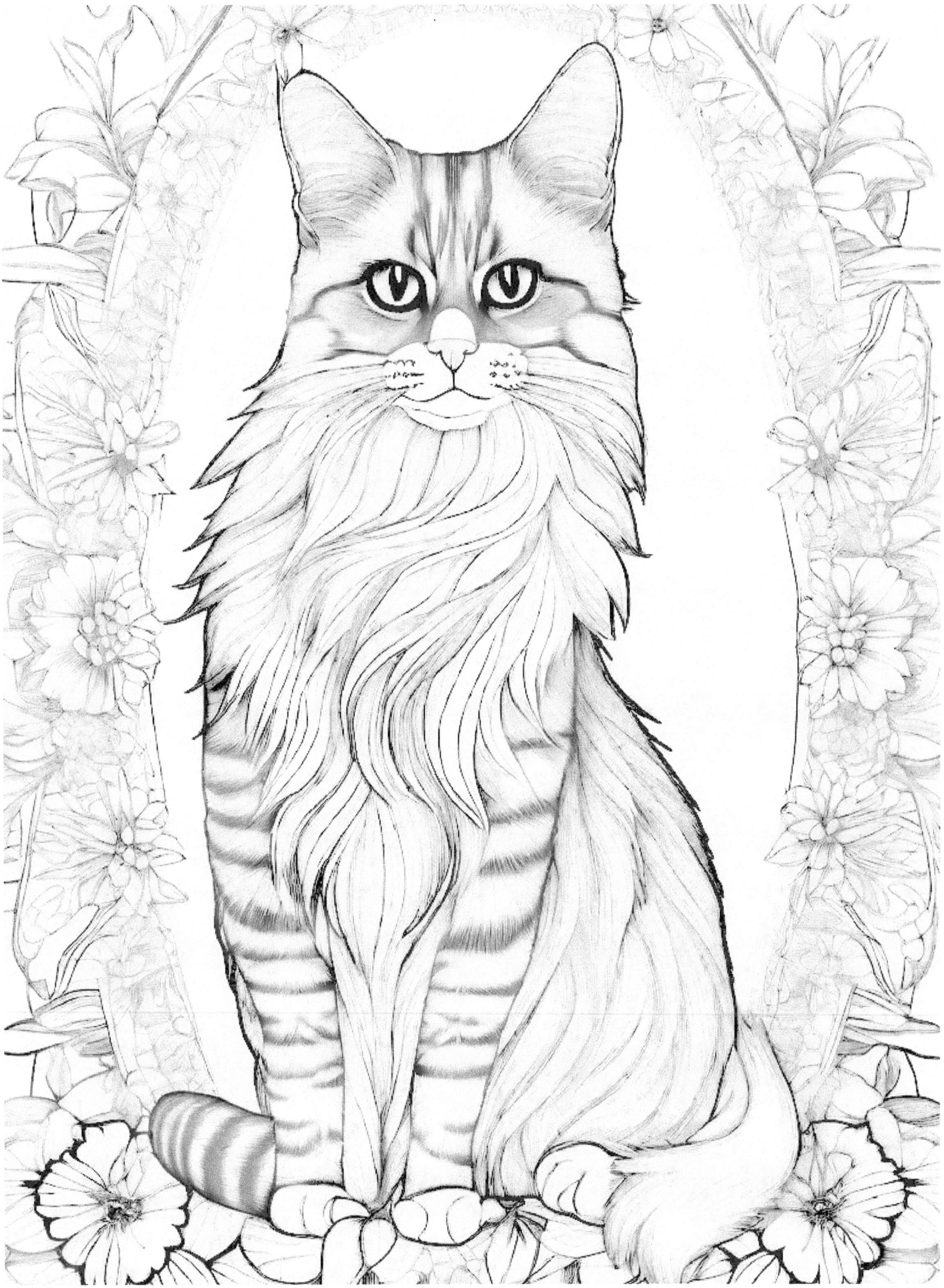

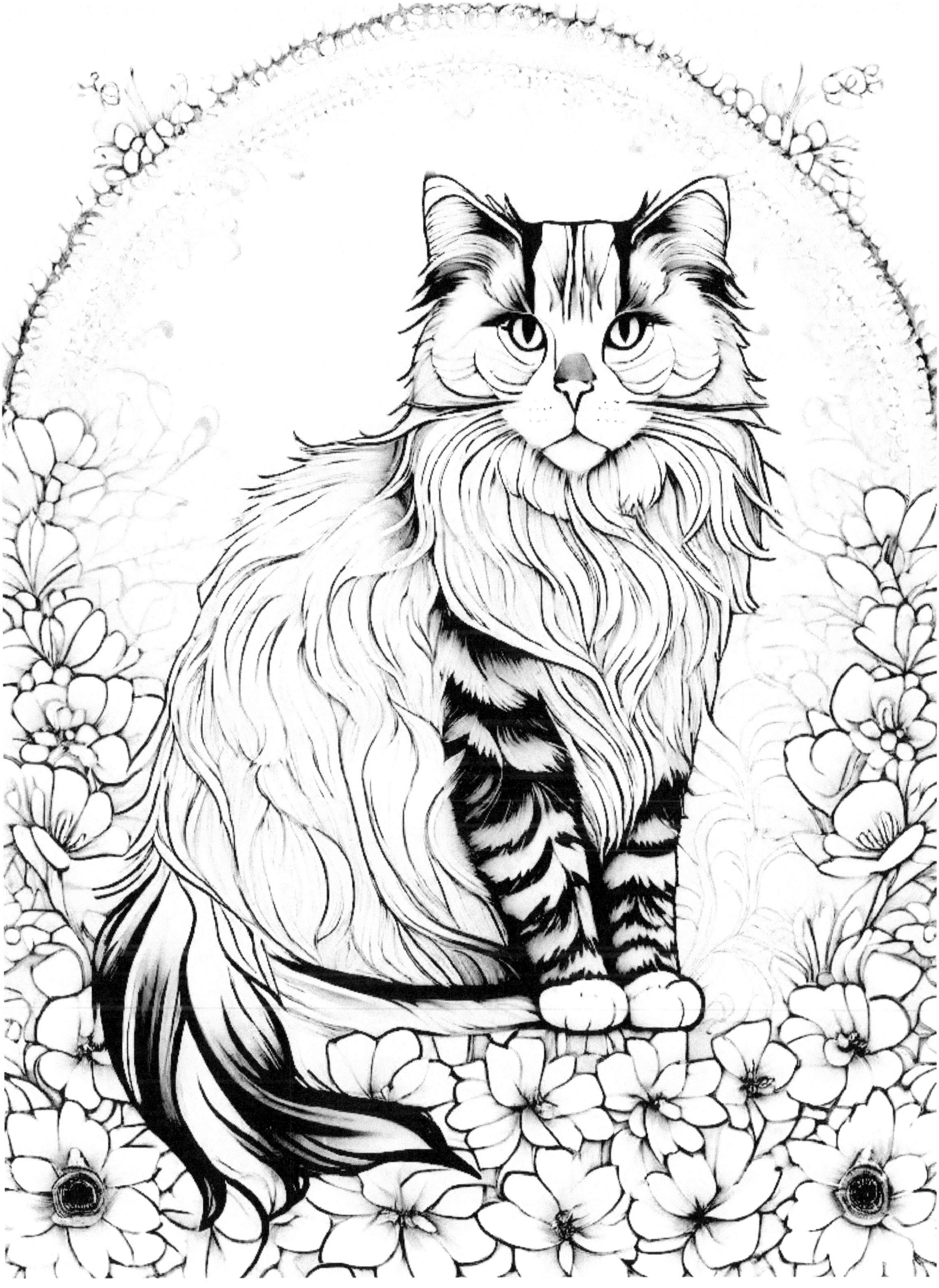

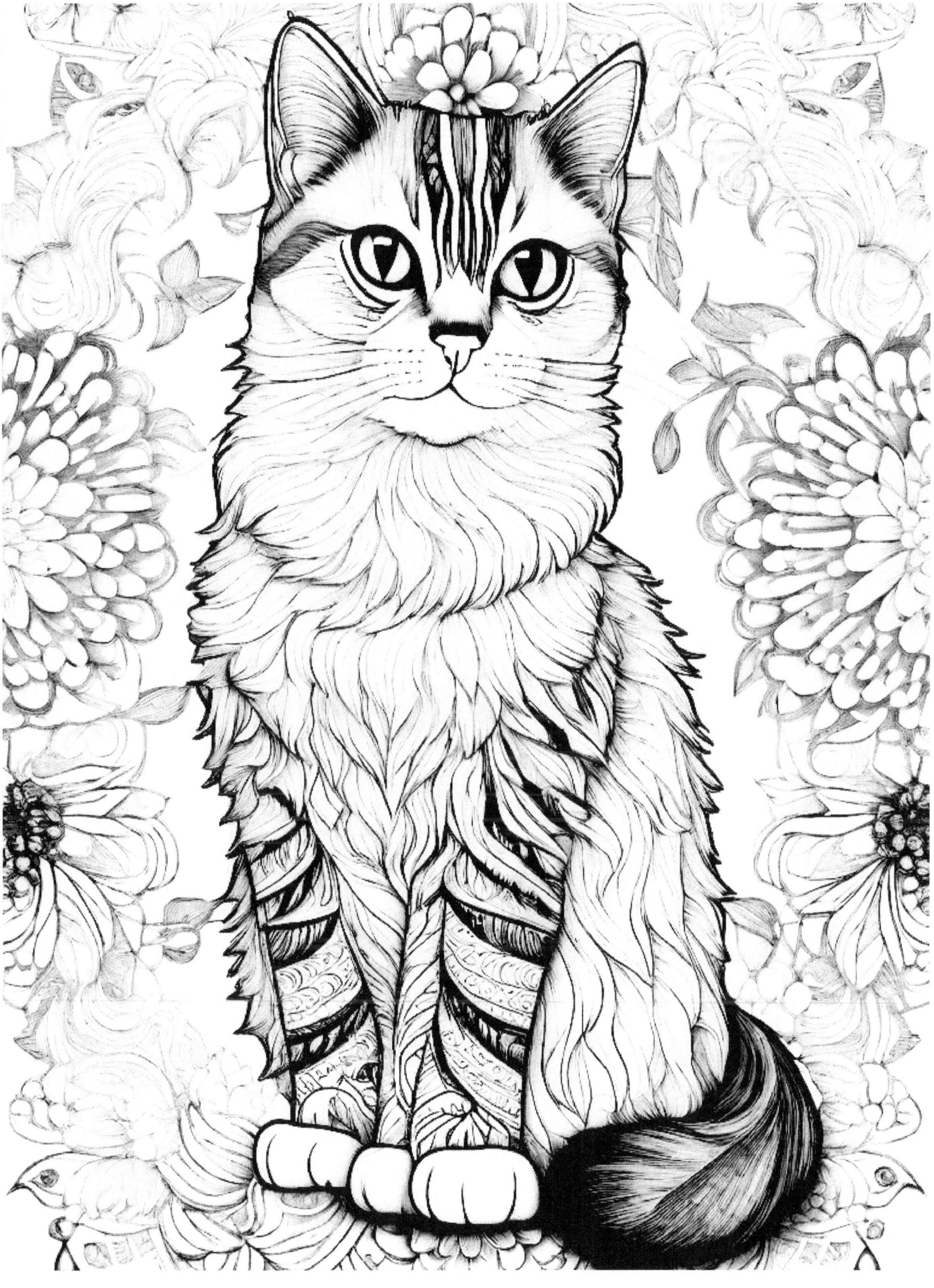

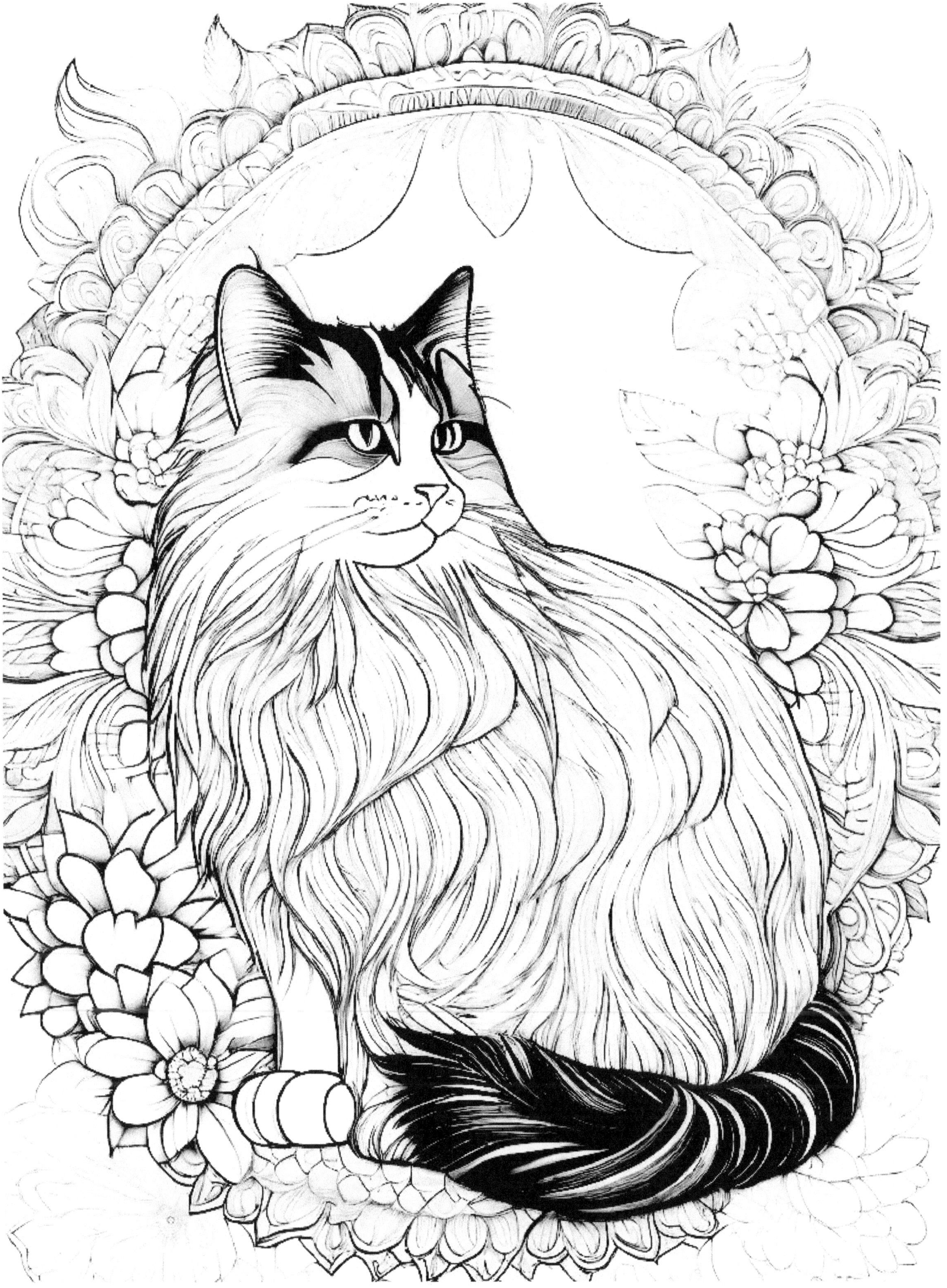

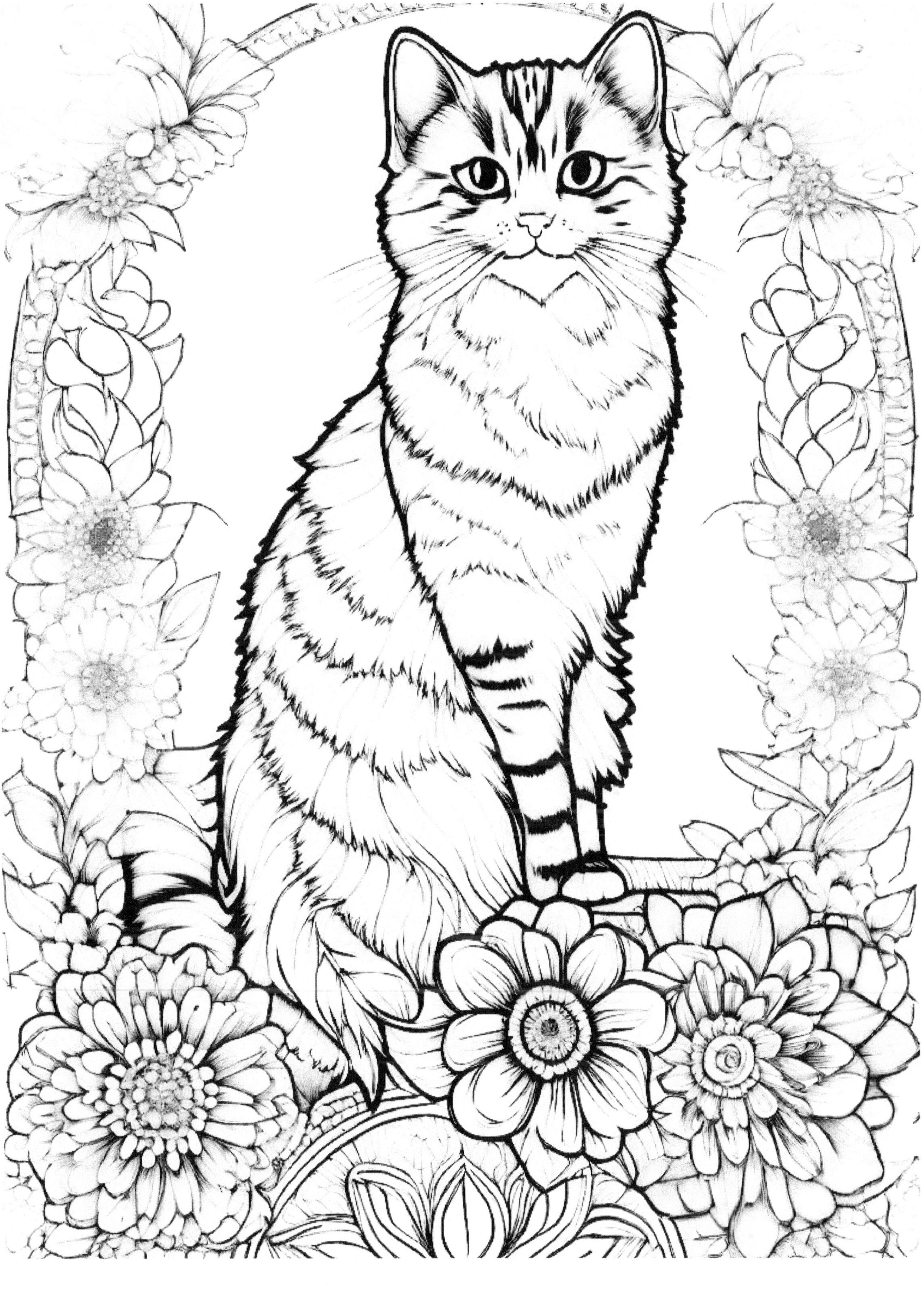

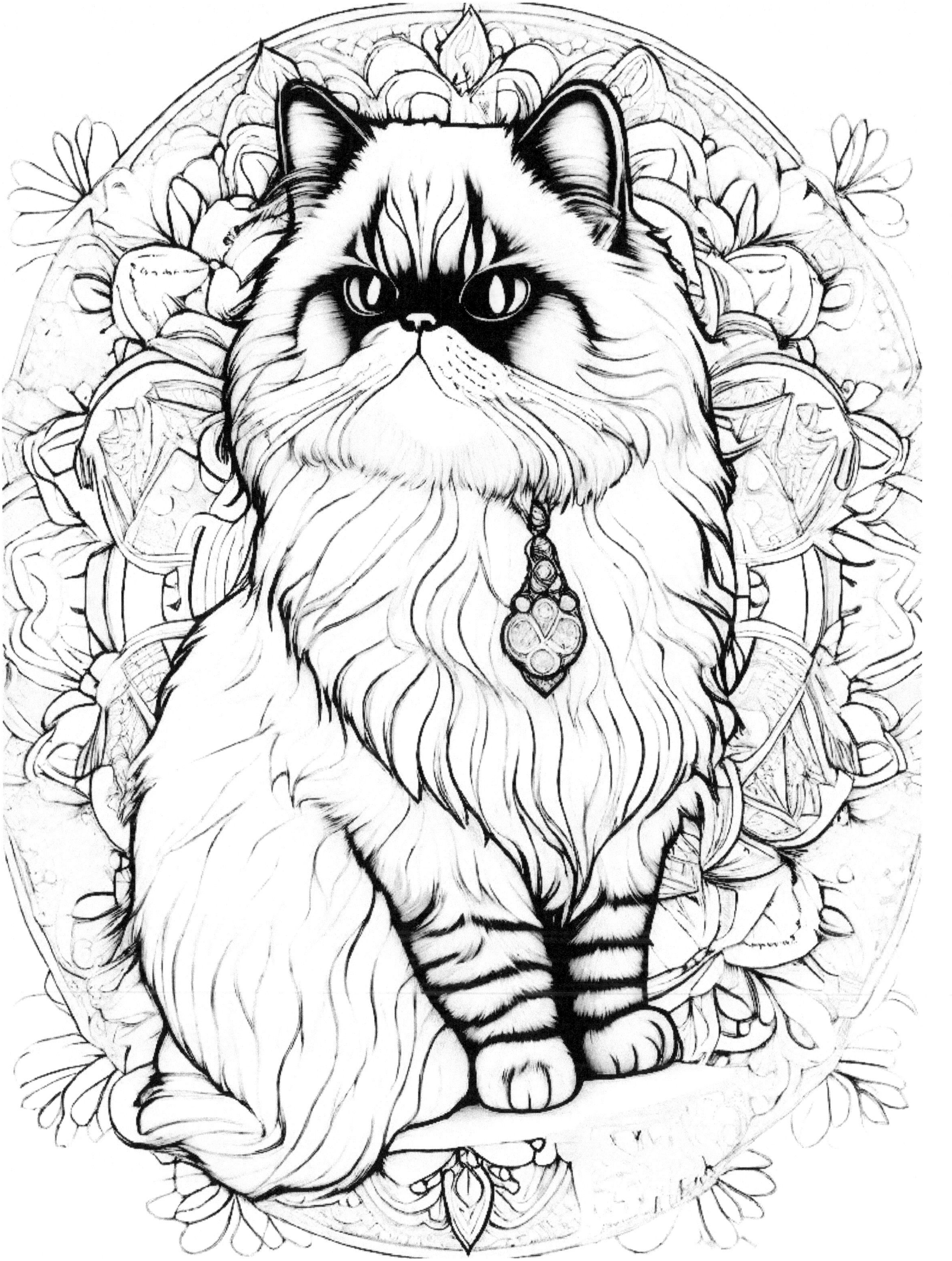

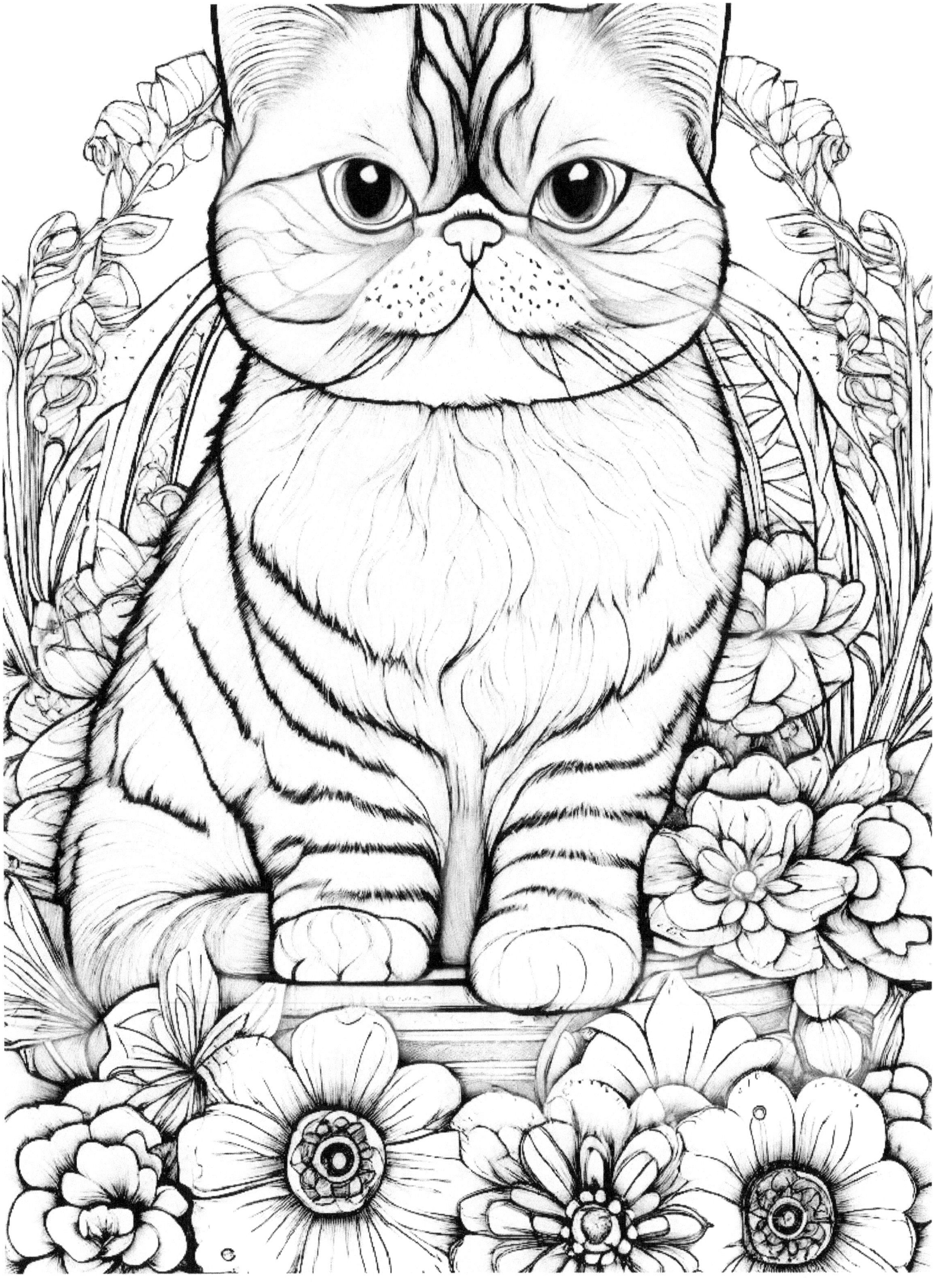

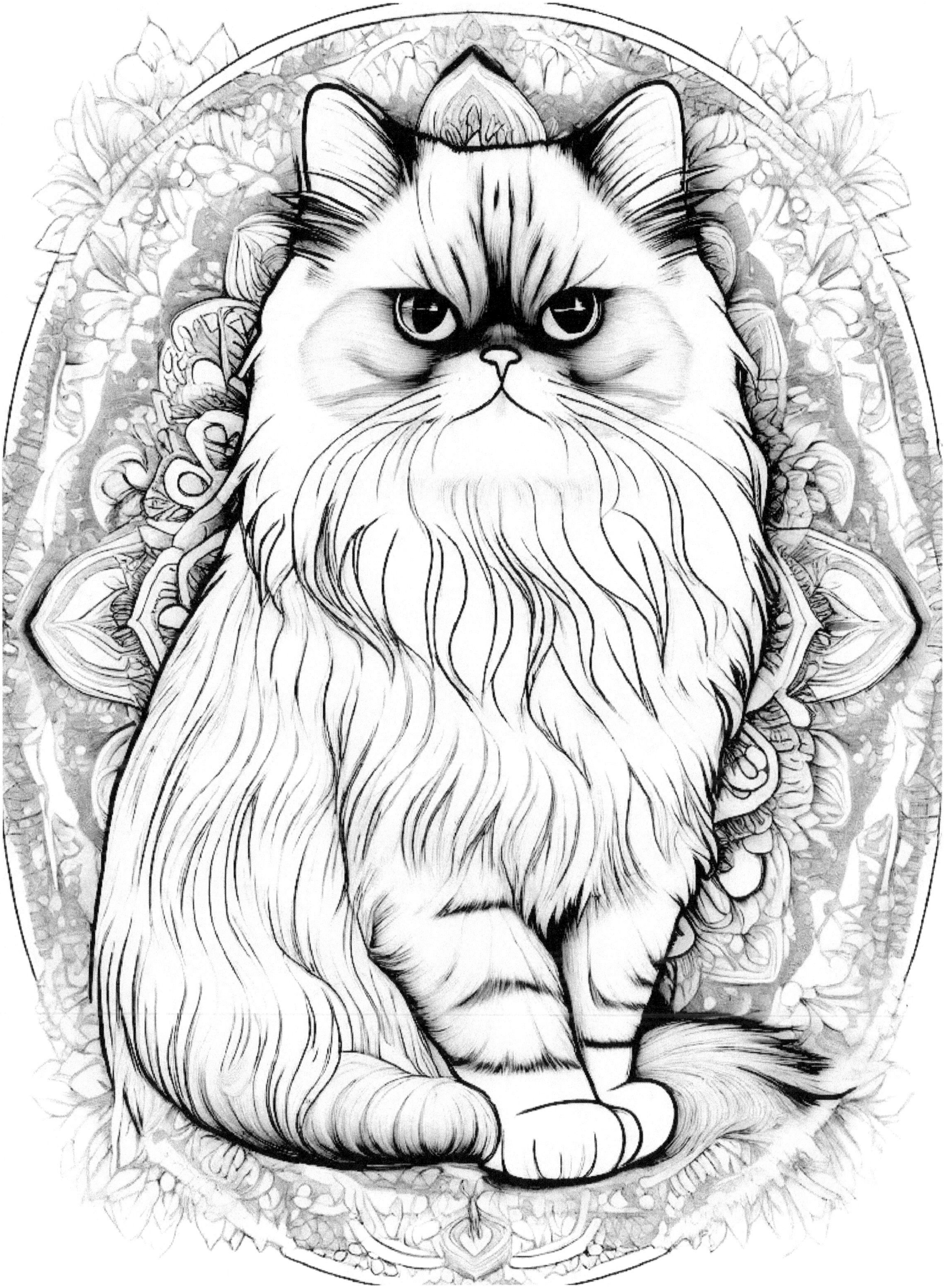

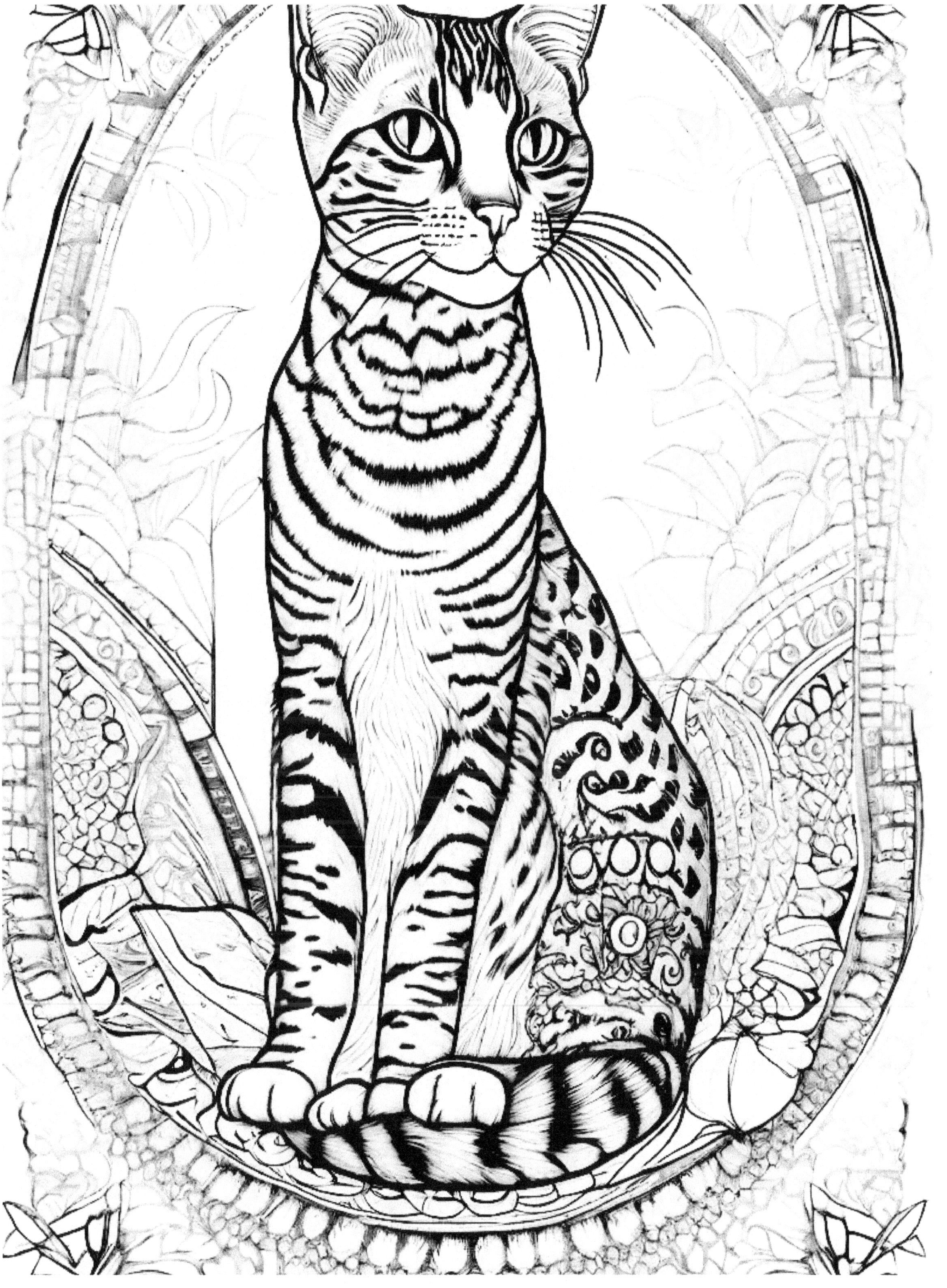

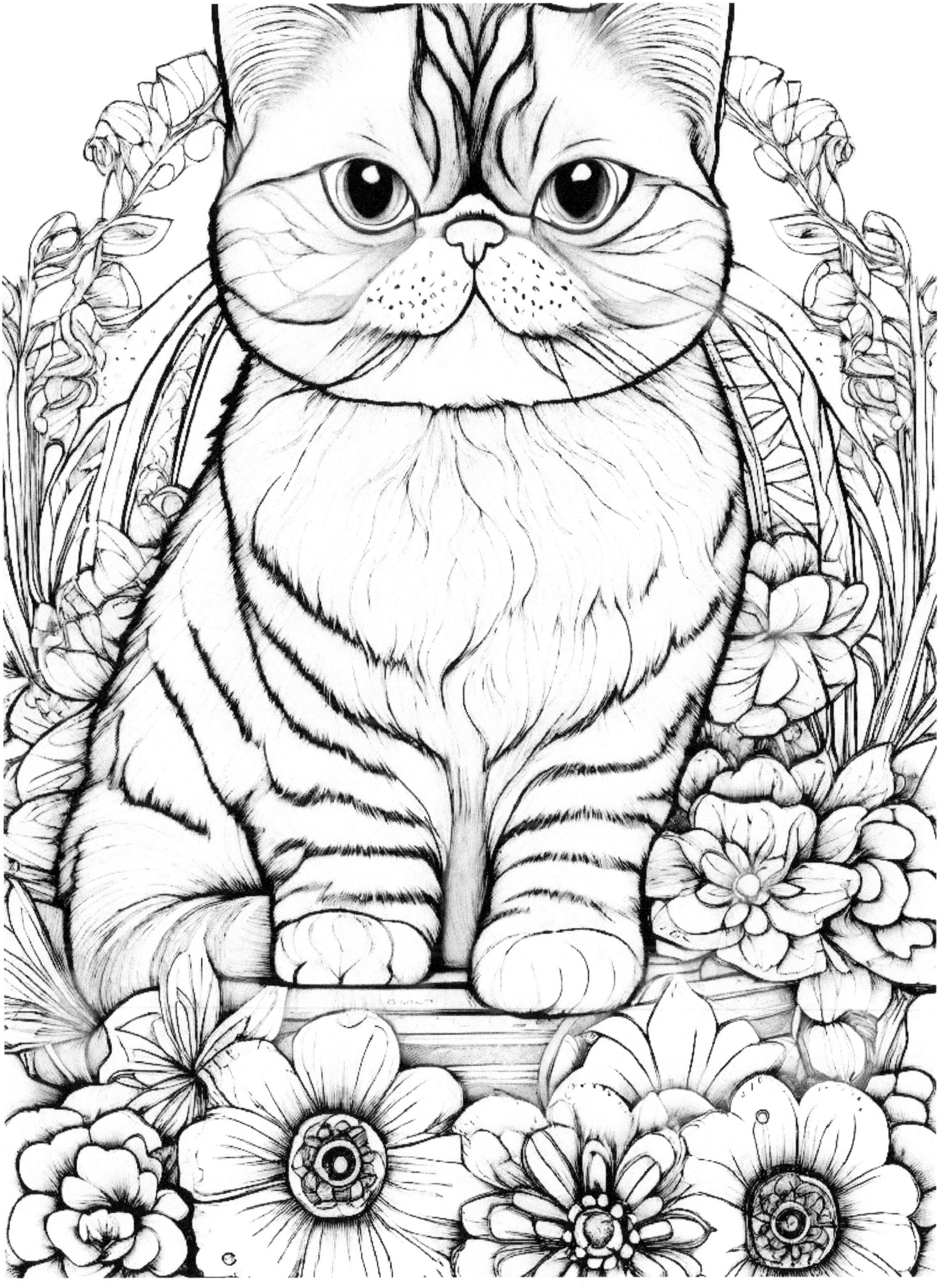

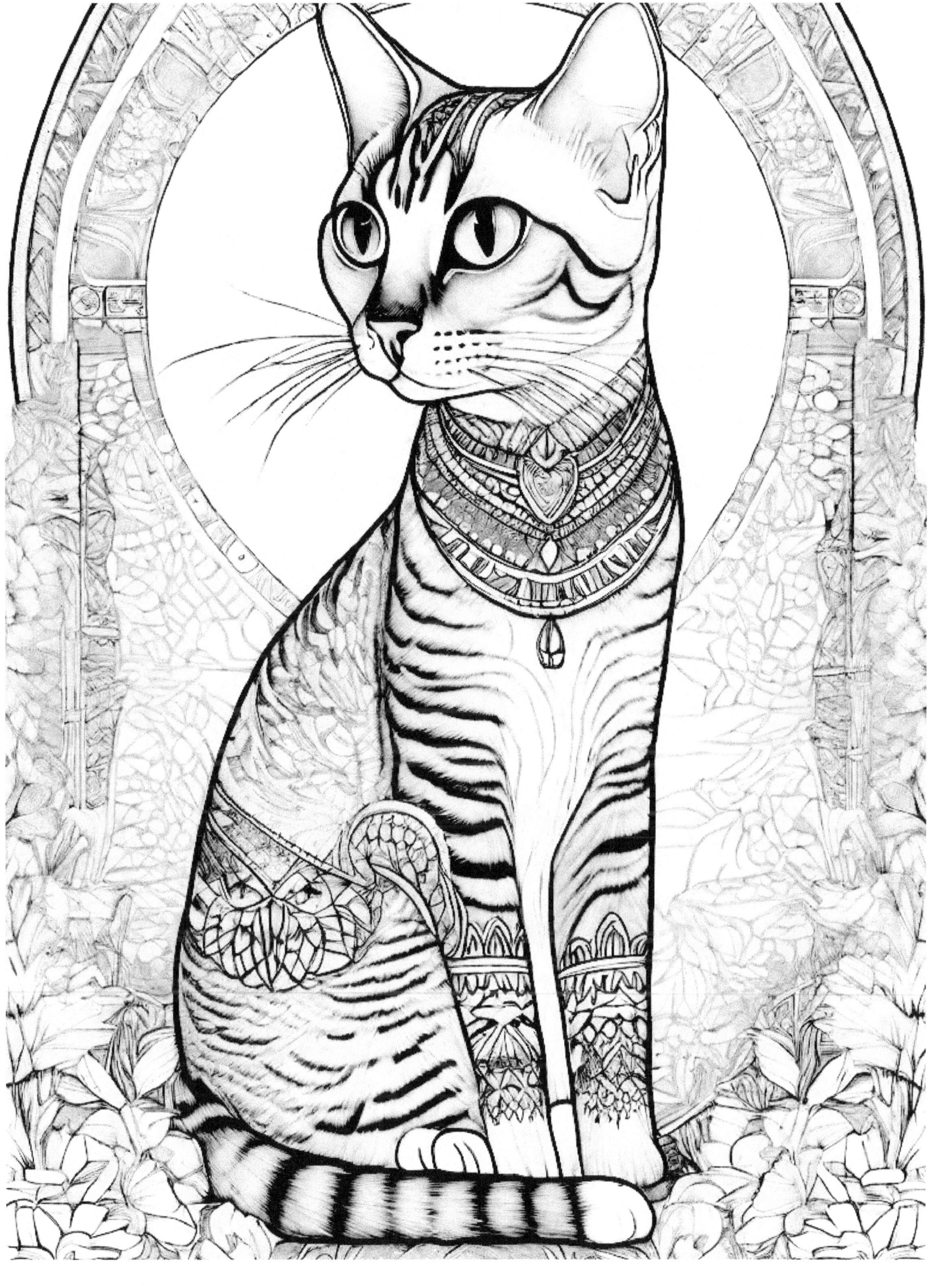

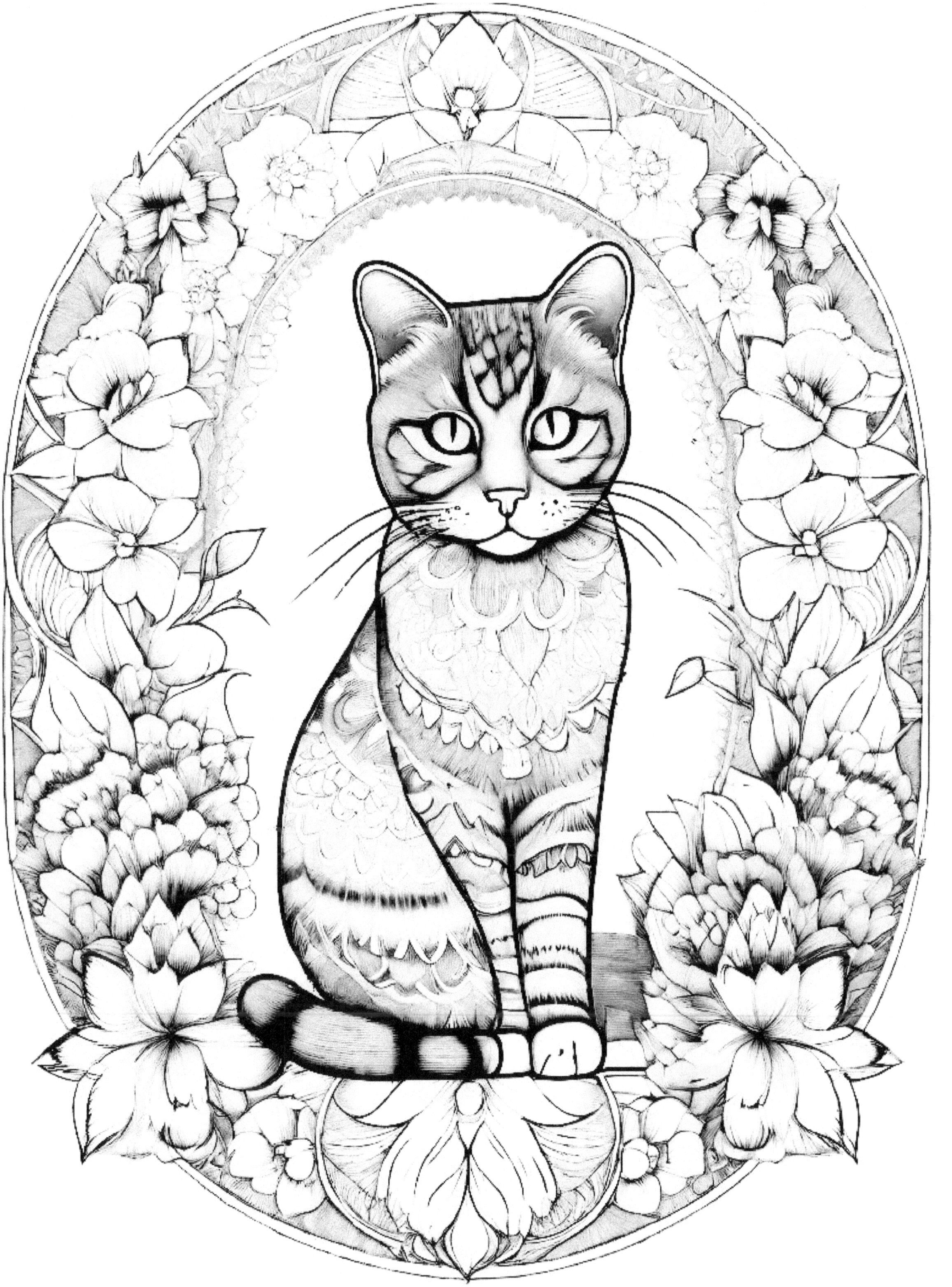

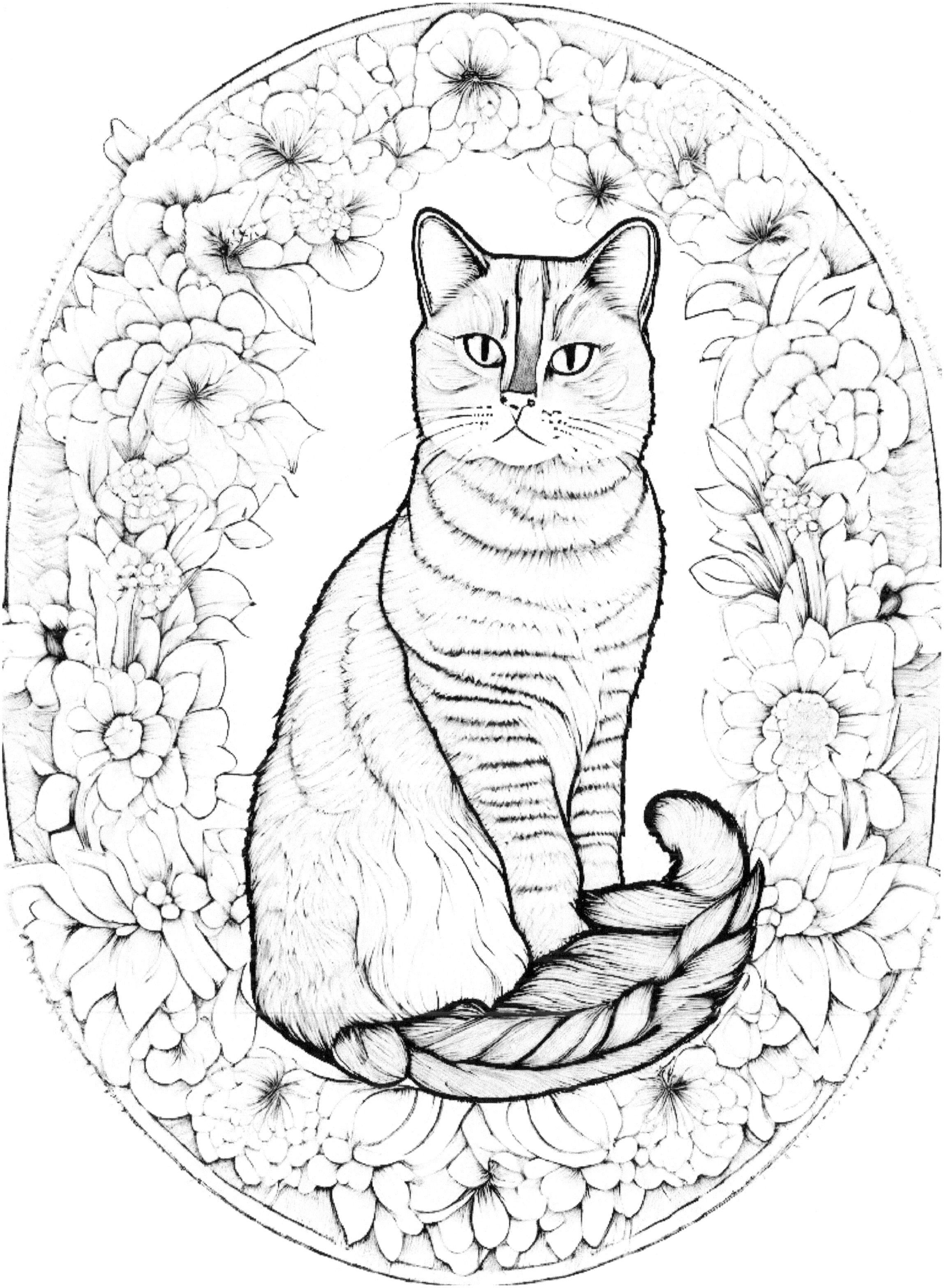

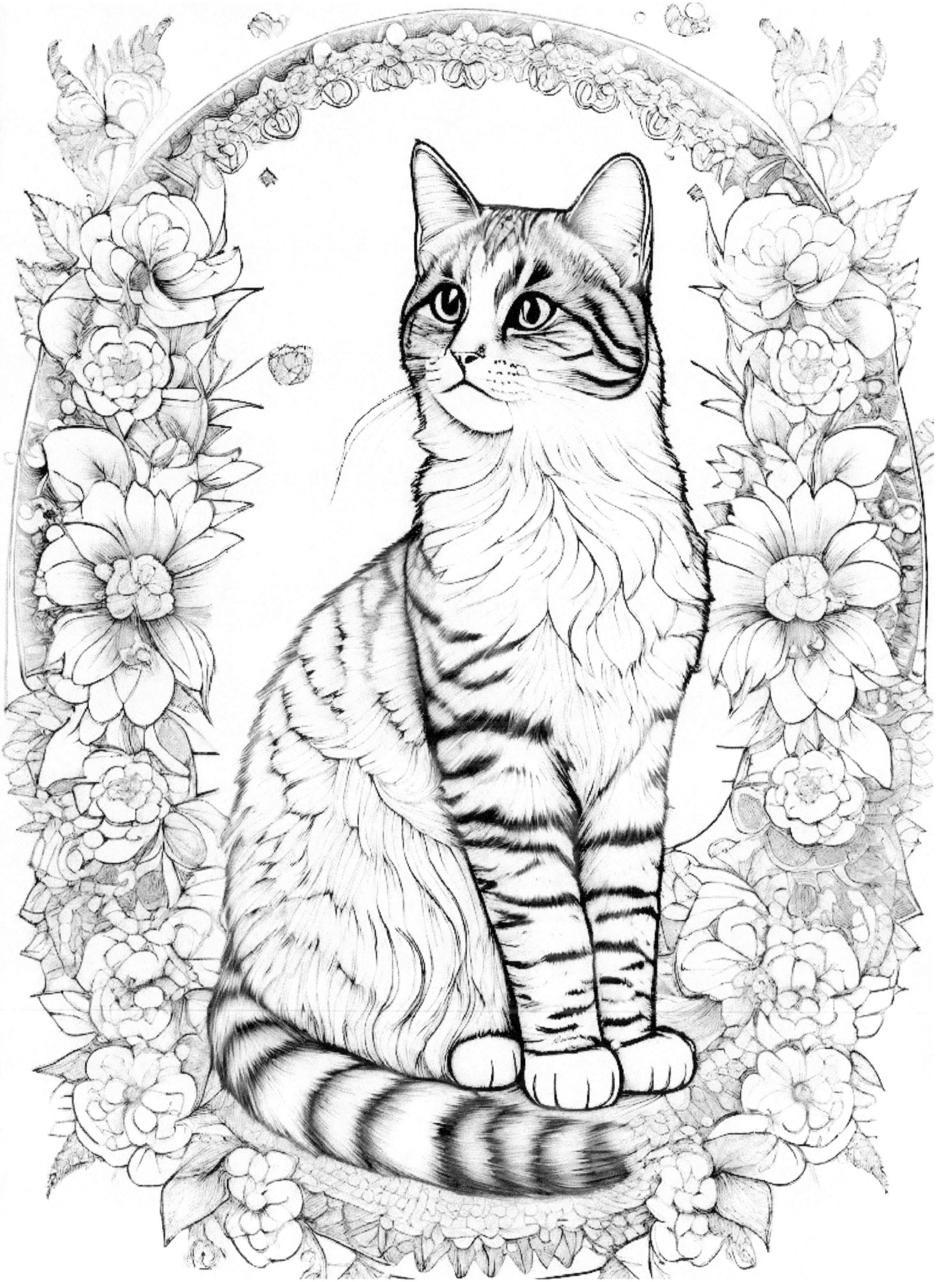

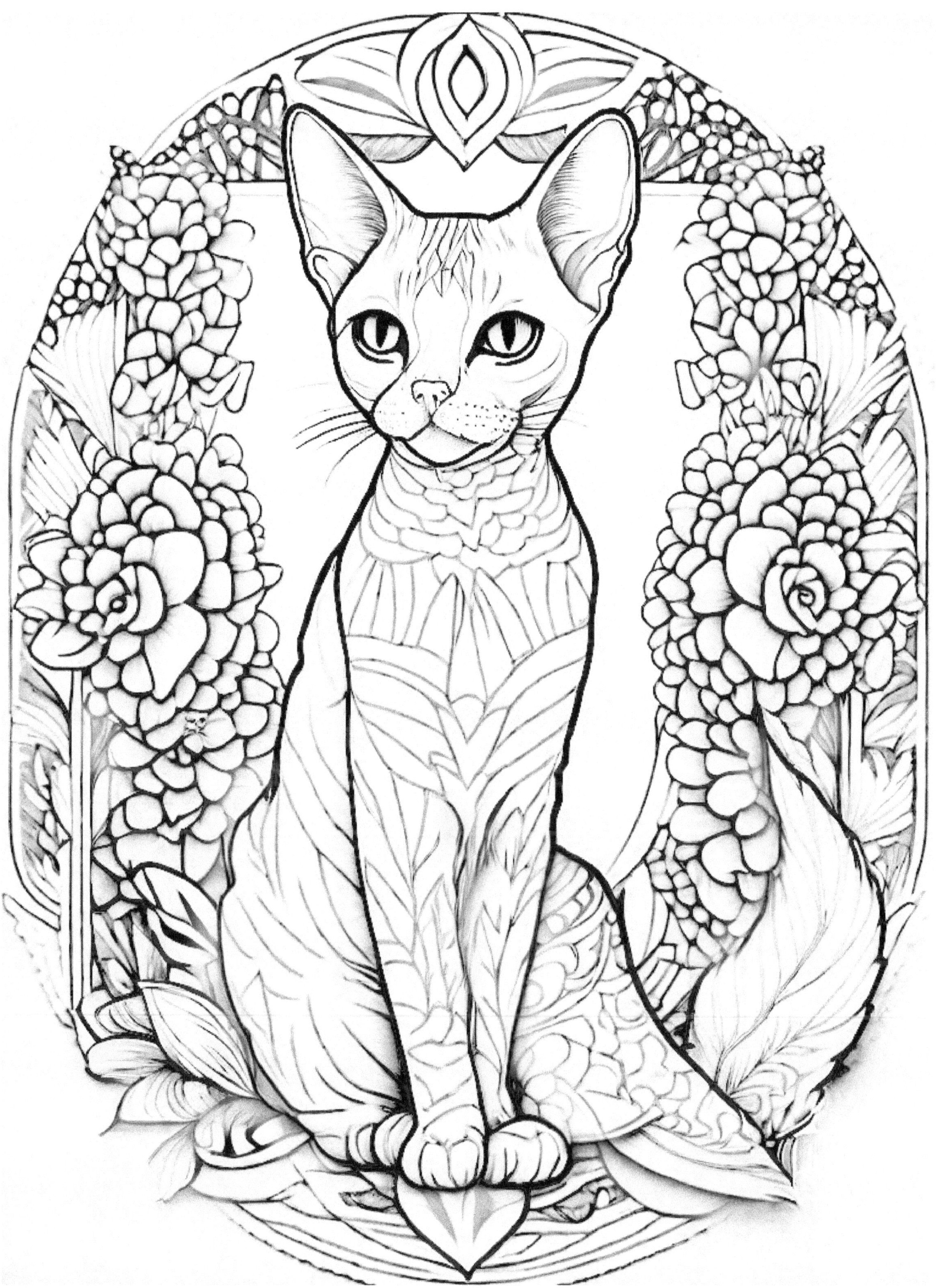

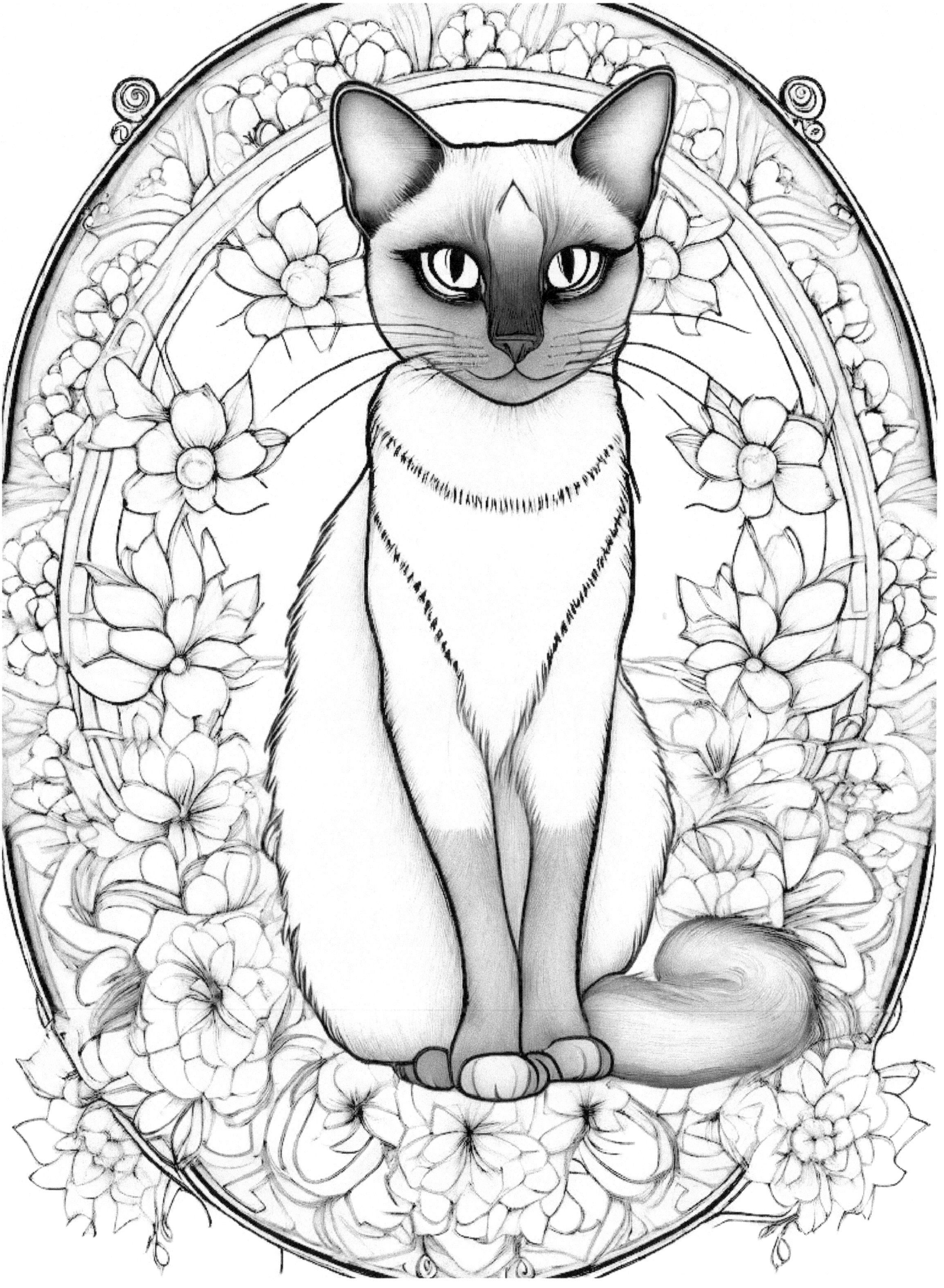

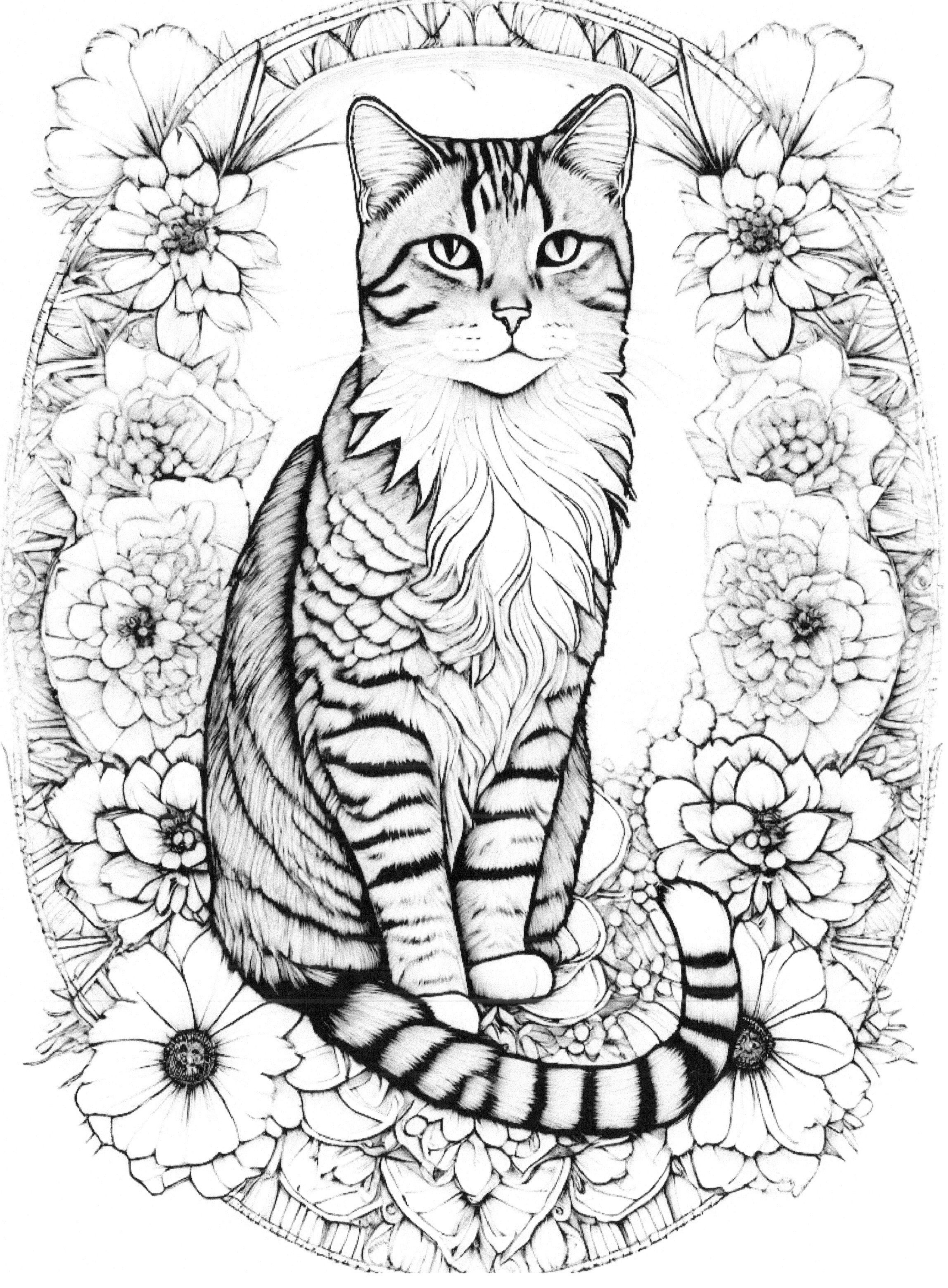

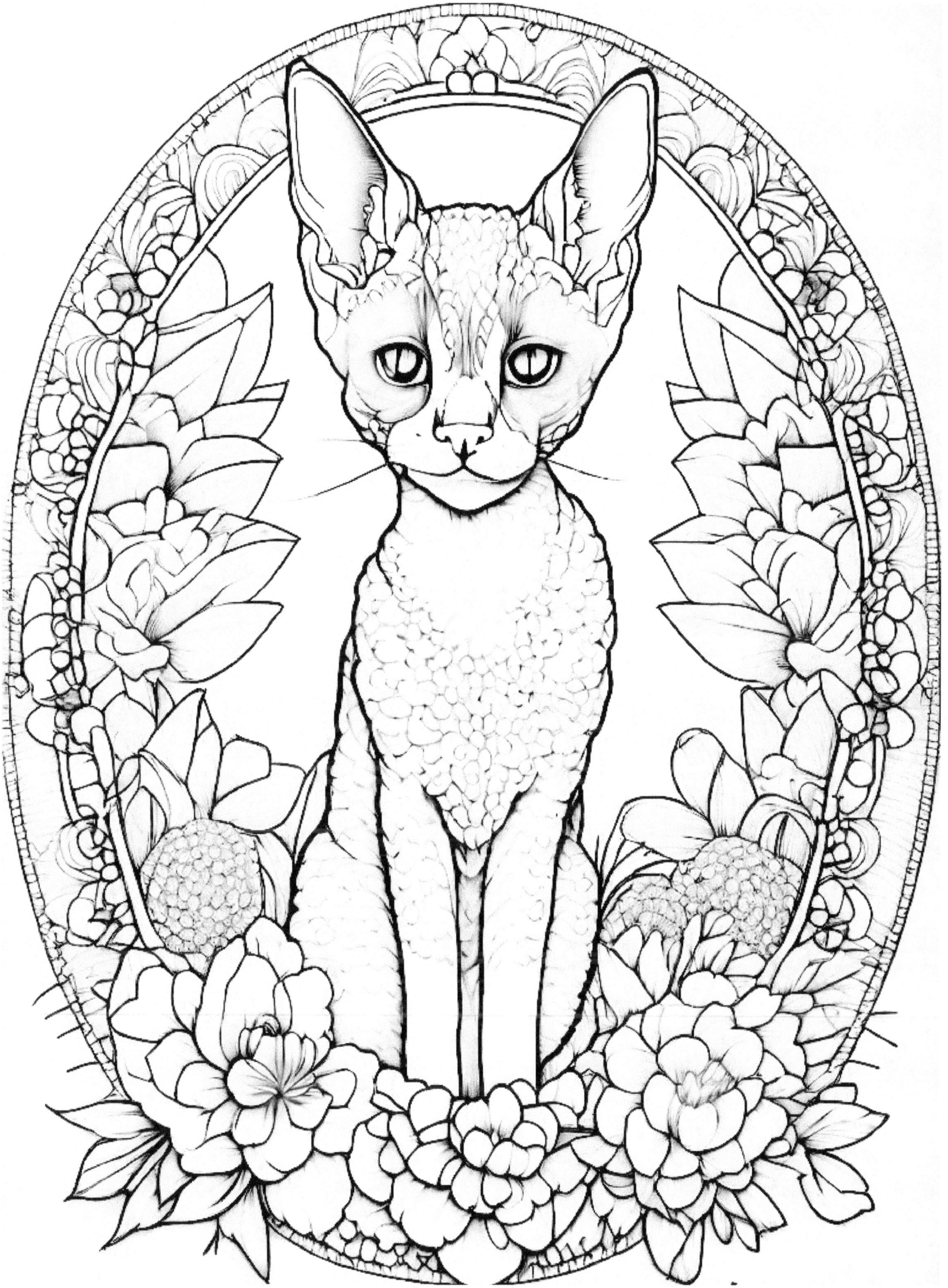

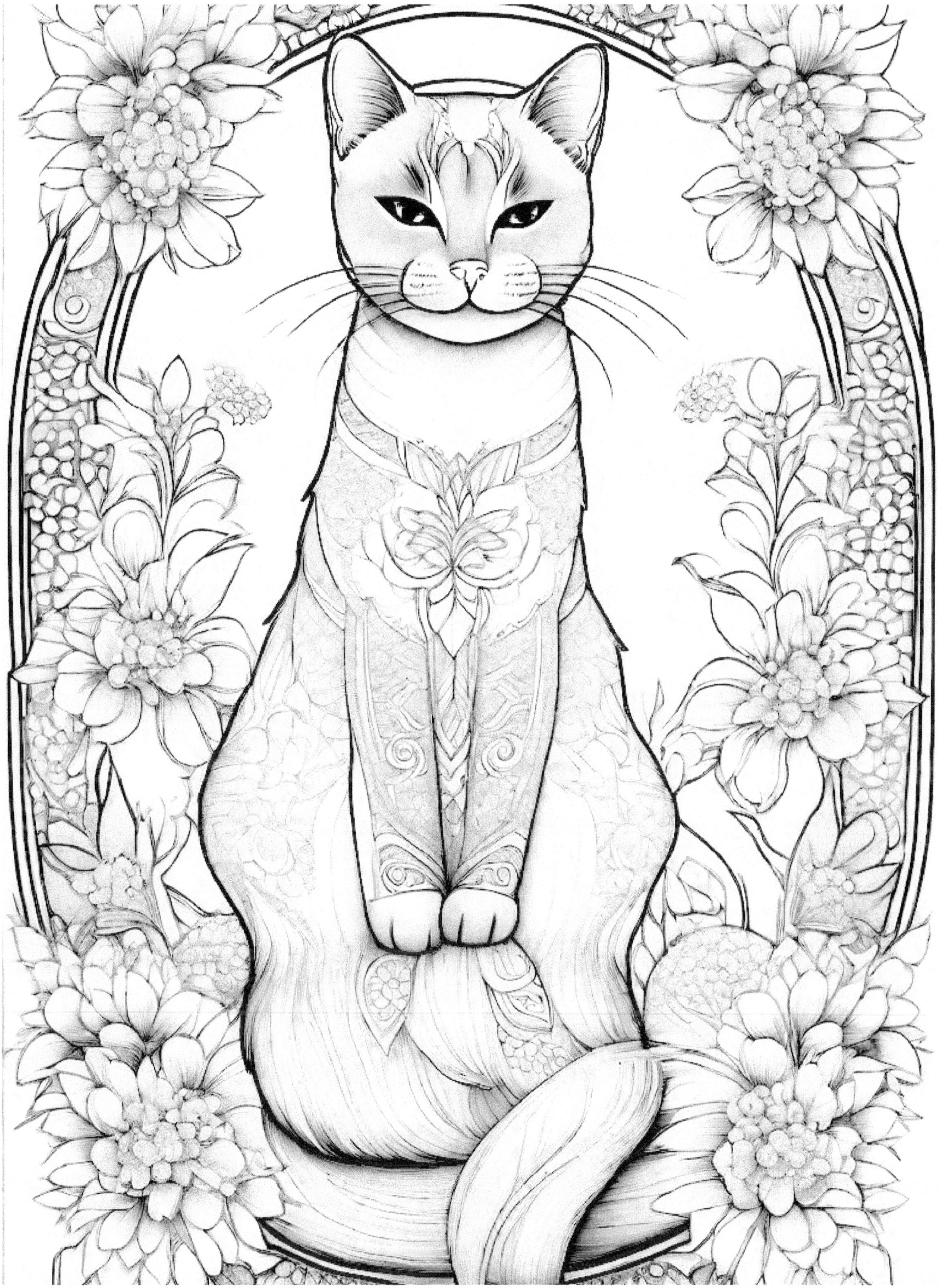

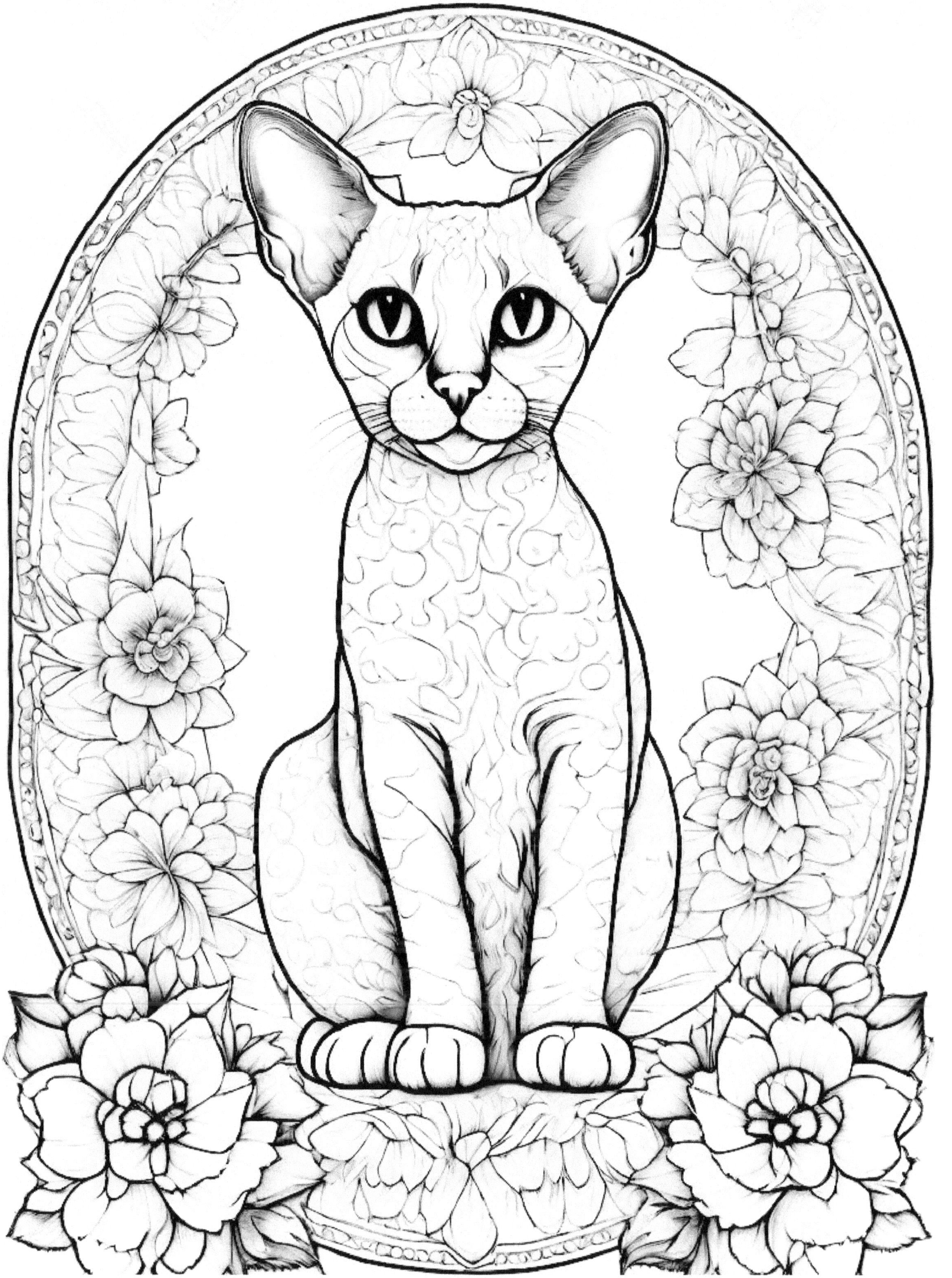

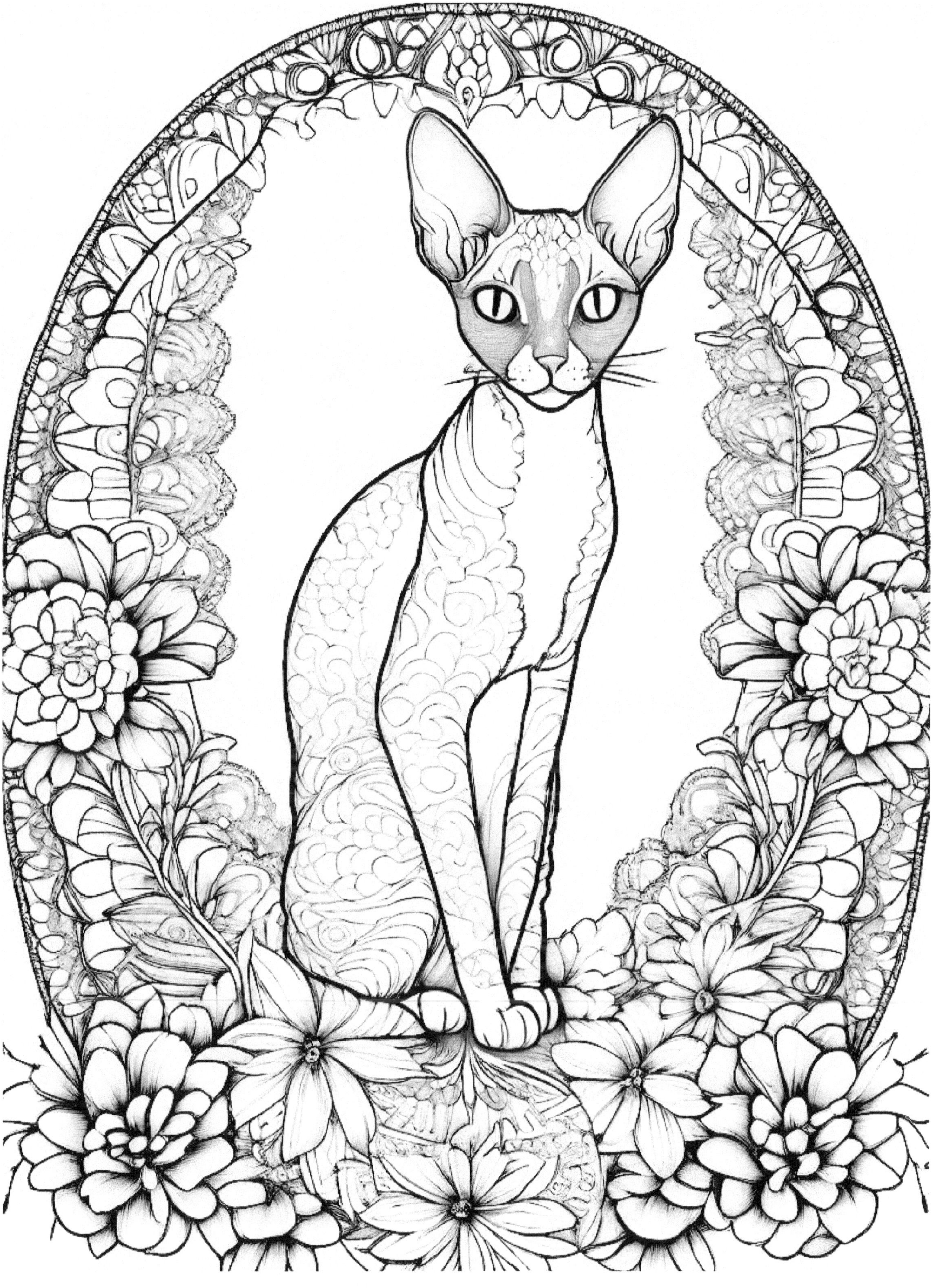

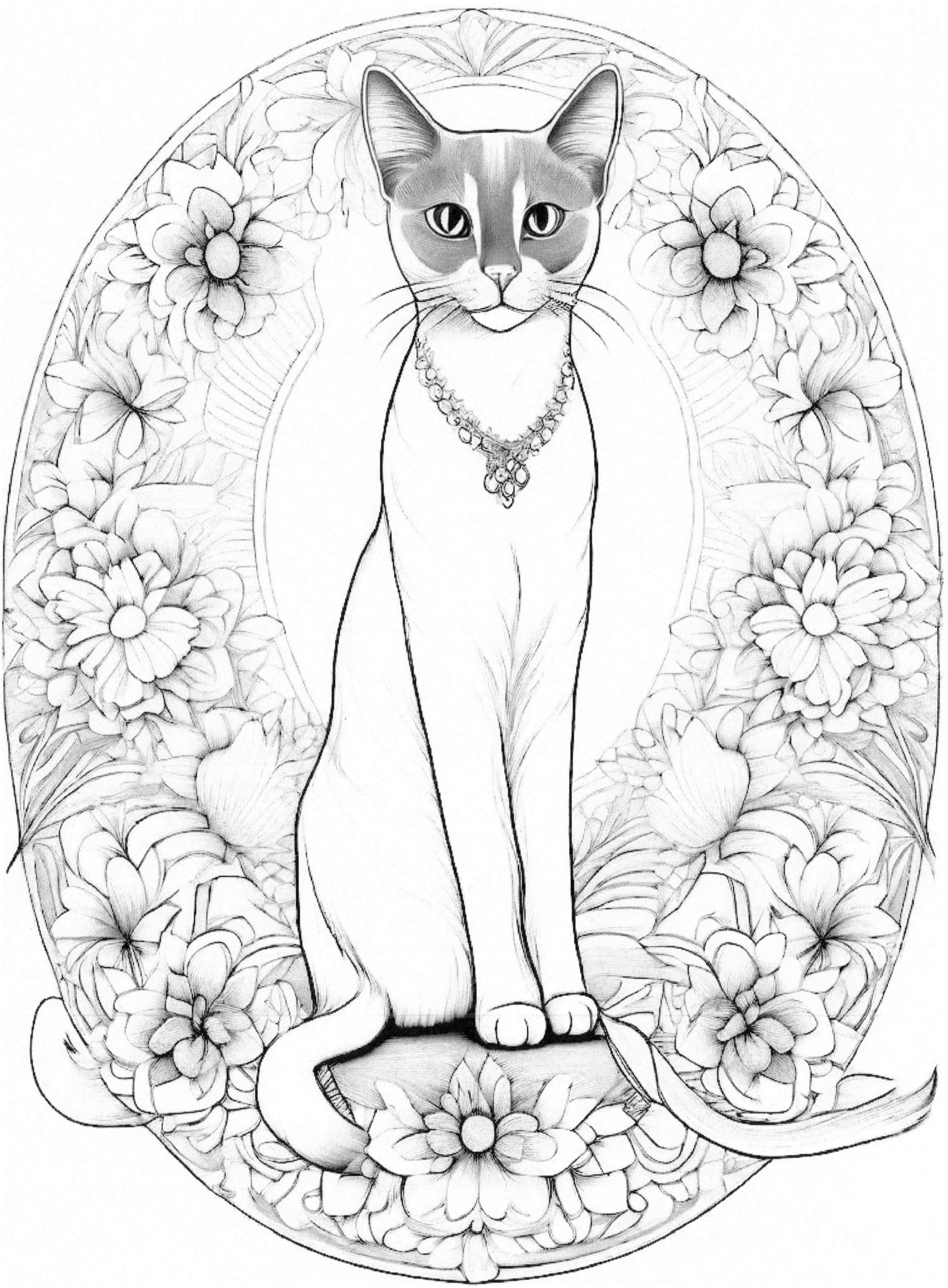

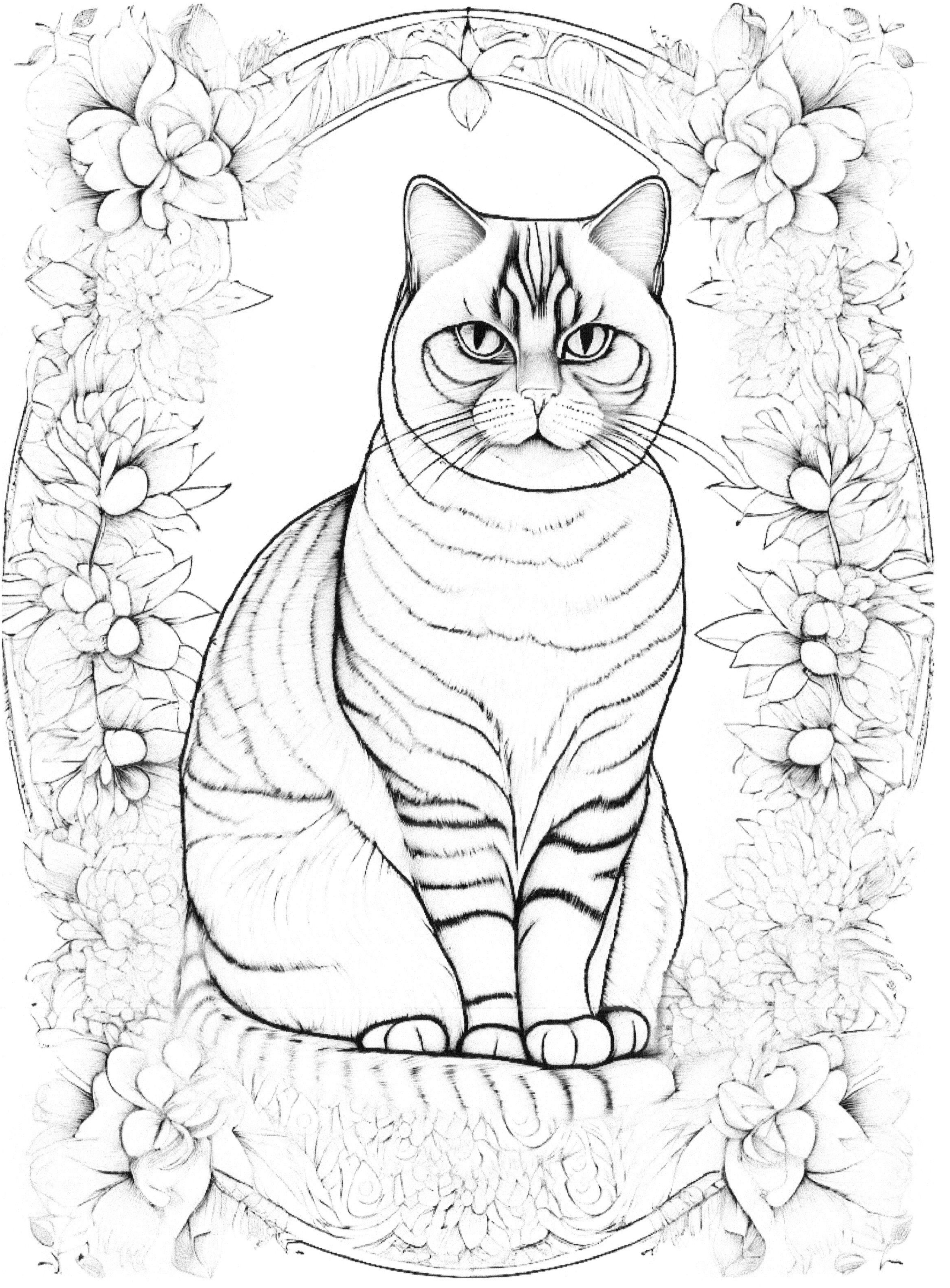

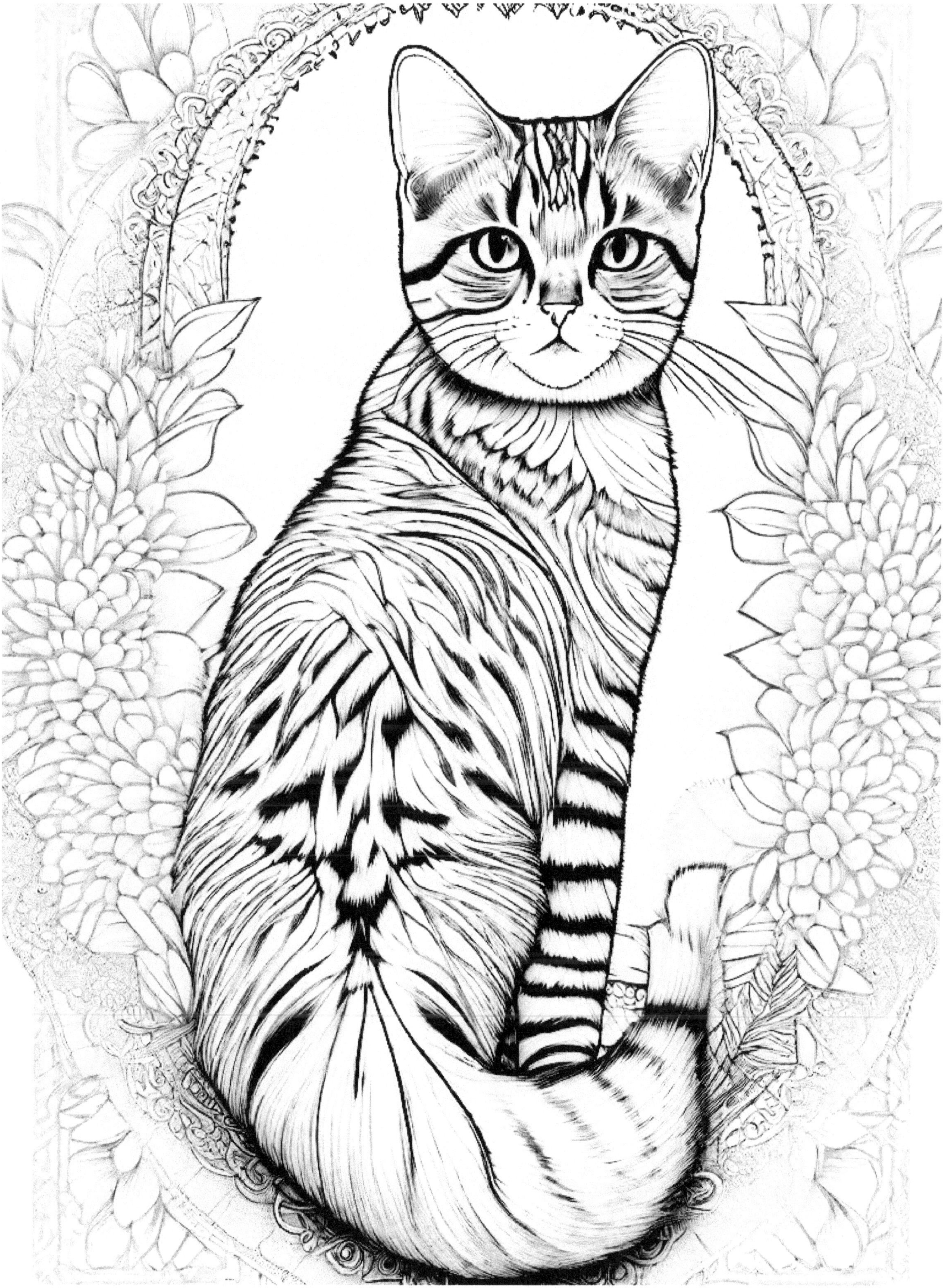

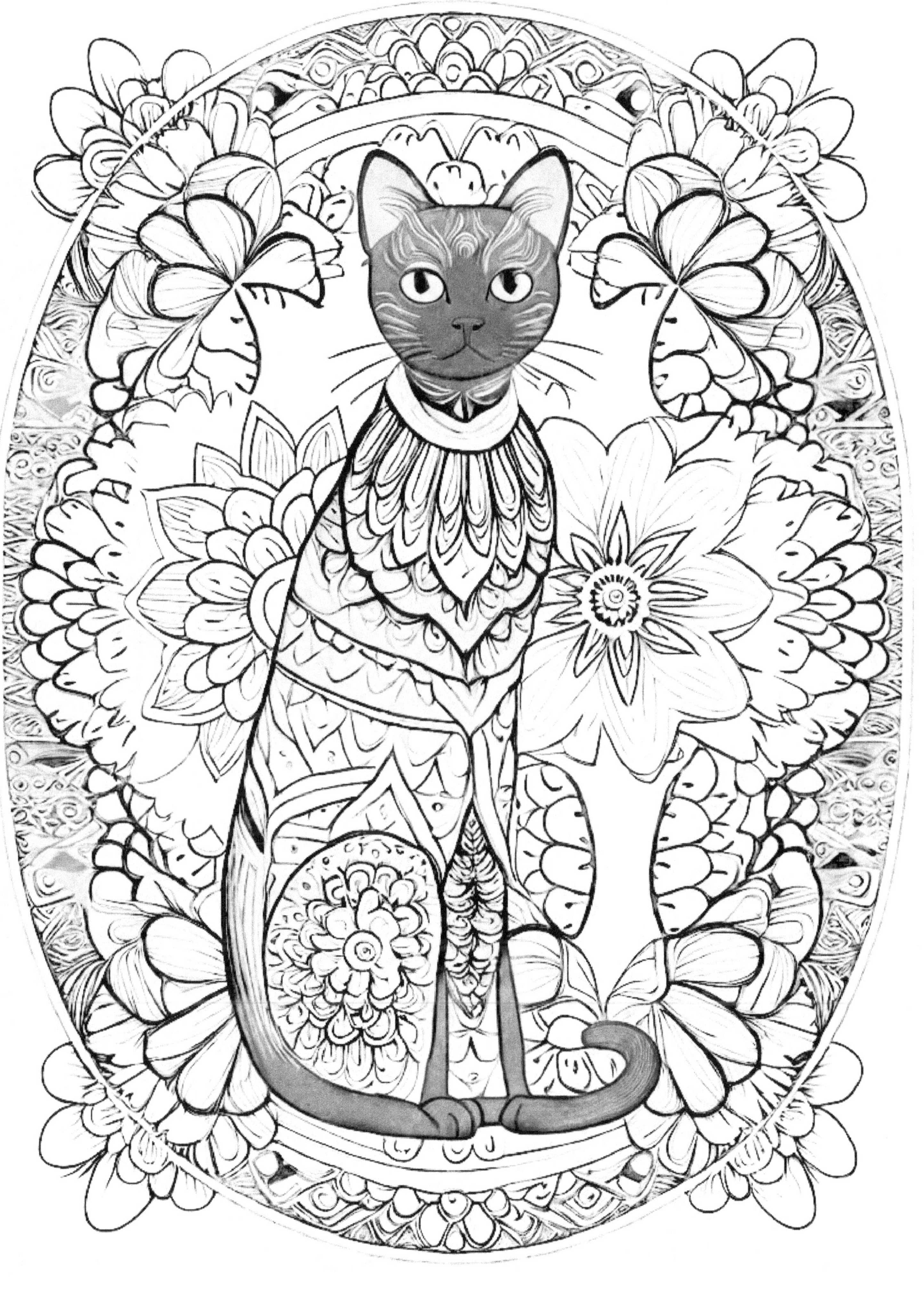

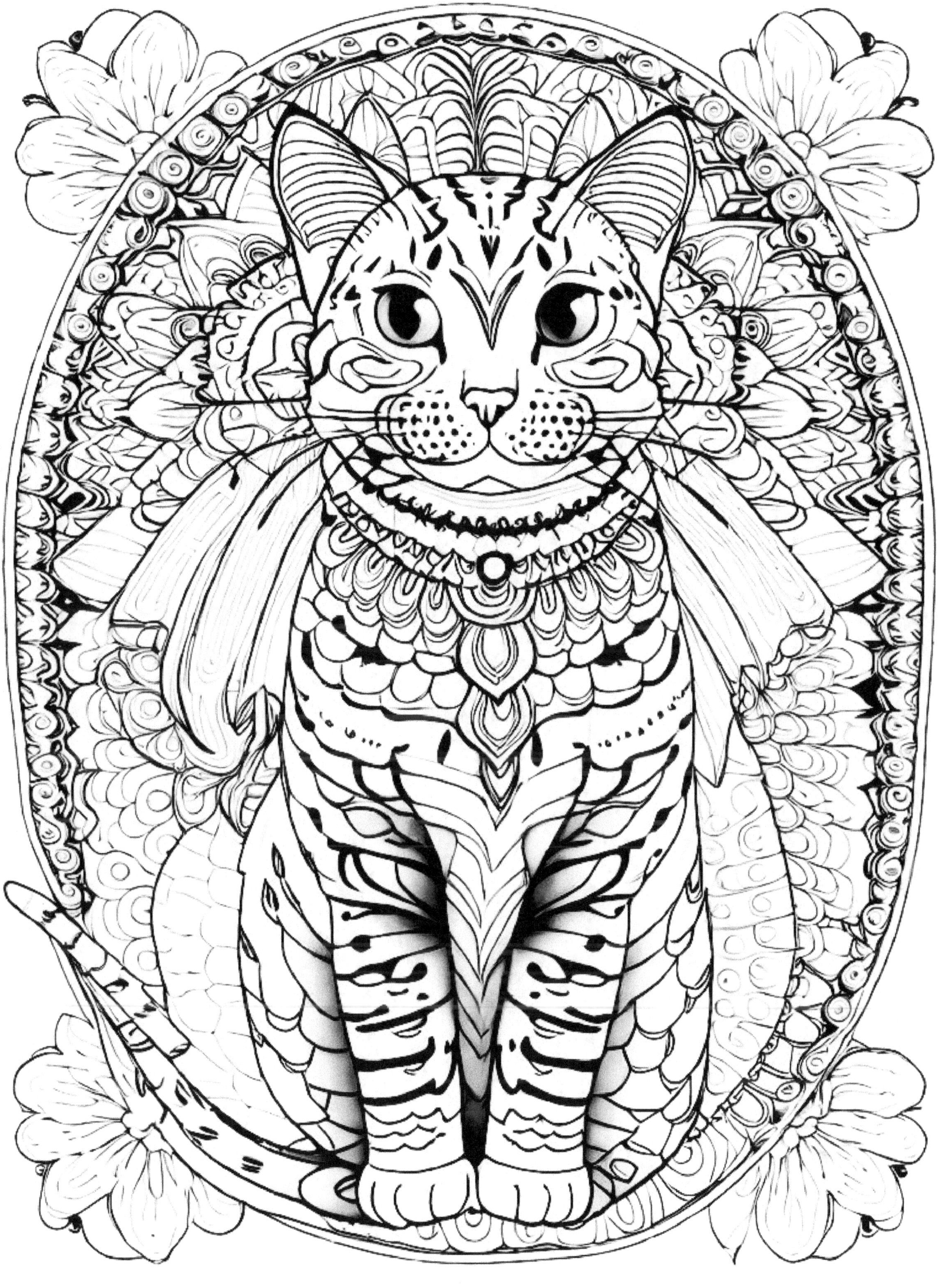

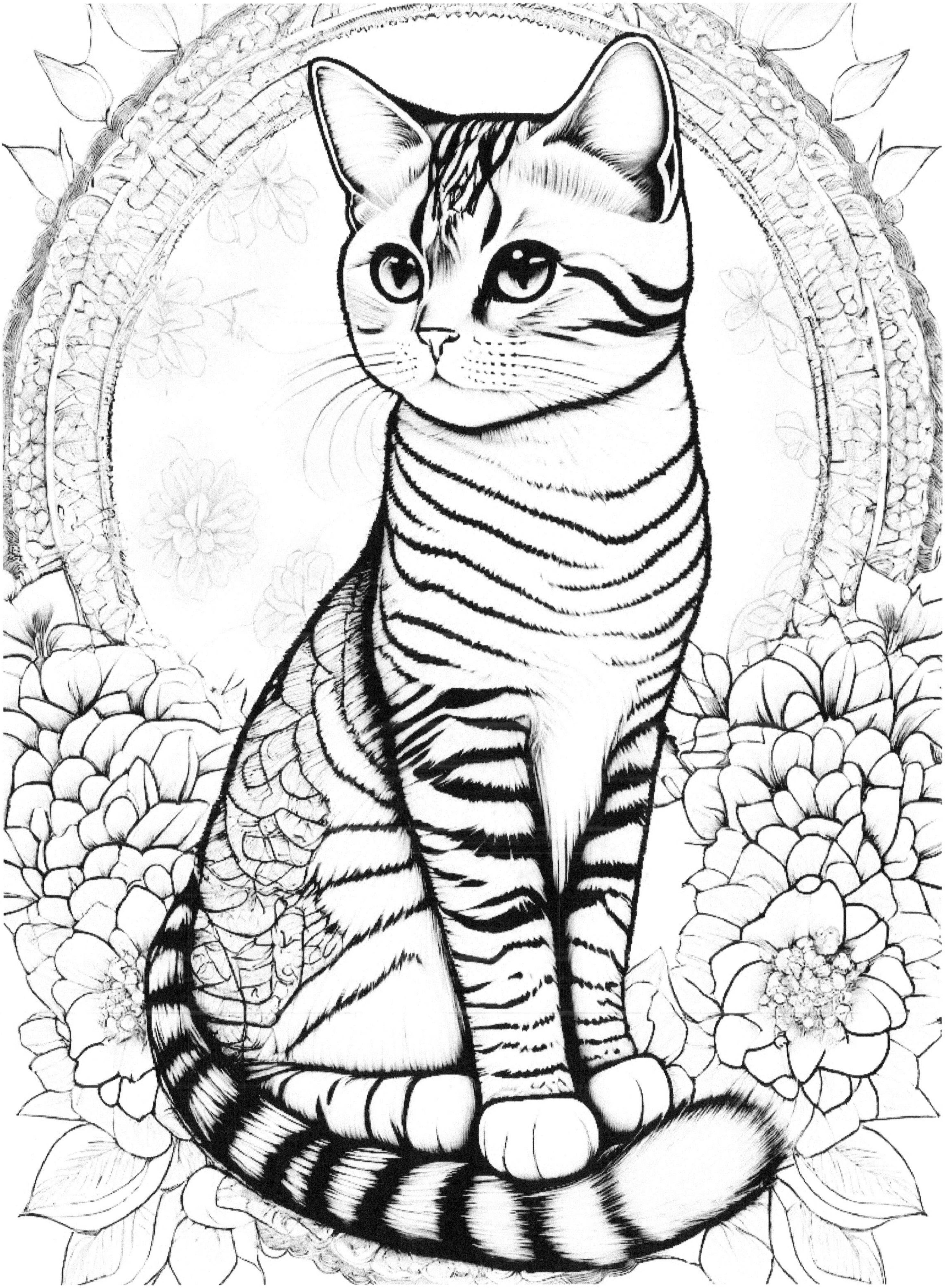

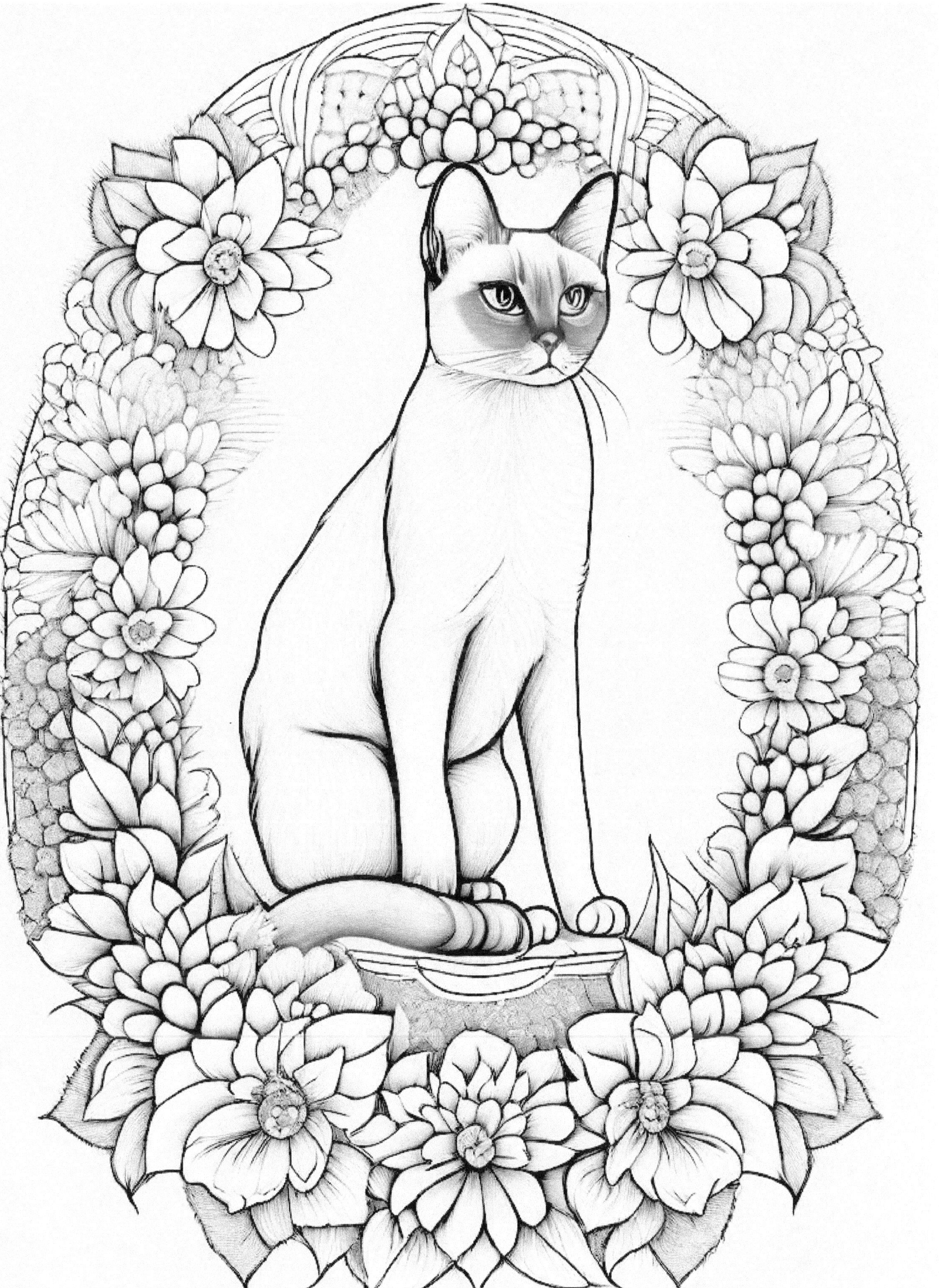

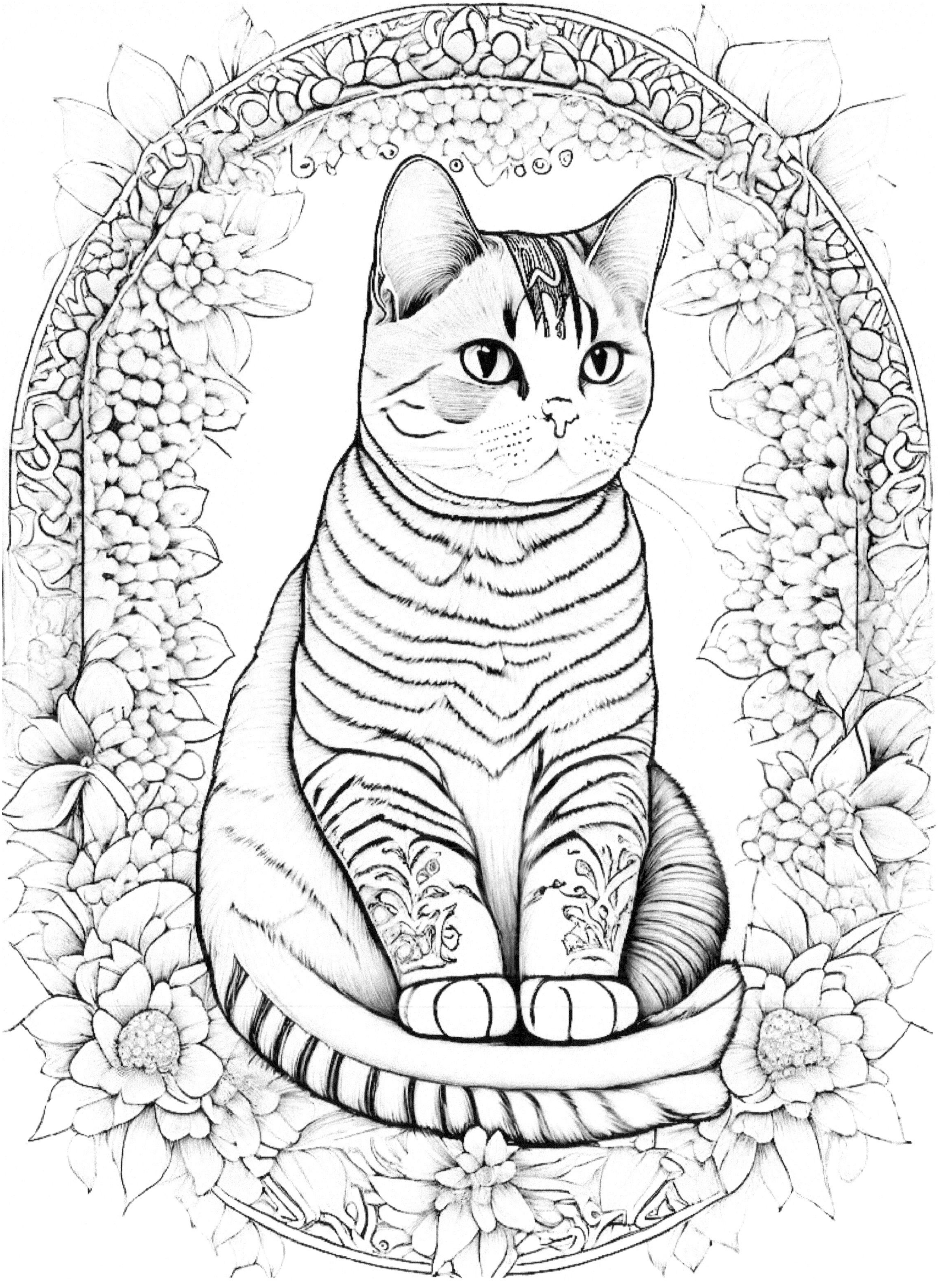

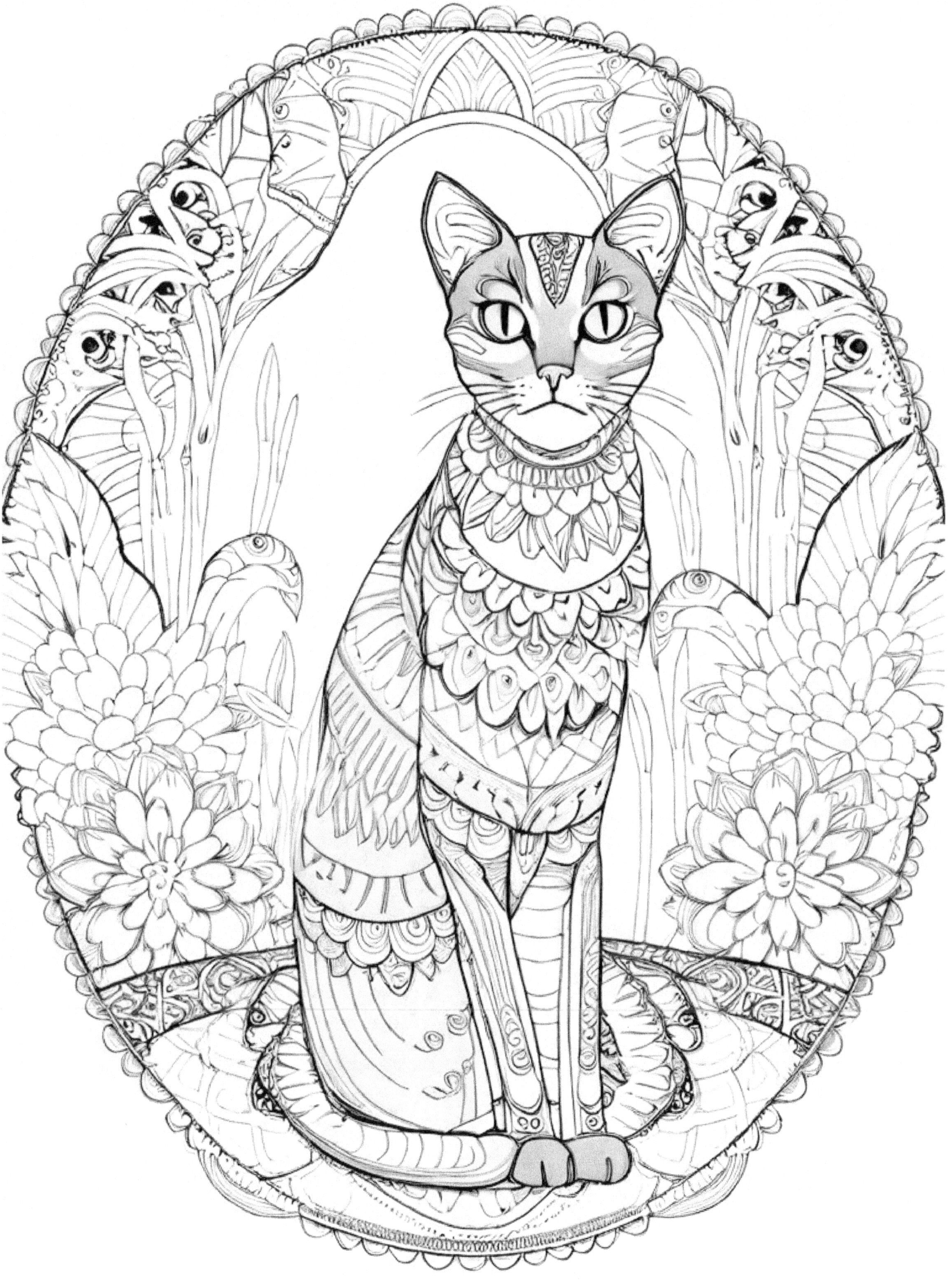

www.ingramcontent.com/pod-product-compliance
Lightning Source LLC
Chambersburg PA
CBHW082139290526
45794CB00008B/3096